To Jackie and Alan,
with love and best wishes,
from
Bohunka.

Cambridge, 7/2/2007.

A Handbook of

# CZECH
# PROSE
# WRITING
1940–2005

The Writer
From Jiří Jirásek, *Unás* (Prager Chronik)

A Handbook of

# CZECH PROSE WRITING

## 1940–2005

BOHUSLAVA BRADBROOK

**sussex**
ACADEMIC
PRESS

*Brighton • Portland*

2 4 6 8 10 9 7 5 3 1

*First published 2007 in Great Britain by*
SUSSEX ACADEMIC PRESS
PO Box 139
Eastbourne BN24 9BP

*and in the United States of America by*
SUSSEX ACADEMIC PRESS
920 NE 58th Ave      Suite 300
Portland, Oregon 97213–3786

*British Library Cataloguing in Publication Data*
A CIP catalogue record for this book is available from the British Library.

*Library of Congress Cataloging-in-Publication Data*
Bradbrook, B. R.
A handbook of Czech prose writings : 1940–2005 /
Bohuslava Bradbrook.
   p. cm.
Includes bibliographical references and index.
ISBN 1-84519-173-0 (h/c : alk. paper)
   1. Czech prose literature—20th century—
Handbooks, manuals, etc. 2. Czech prose
literature—21st century—Handbooks, manuals, etc.
I. Title.

PG5010.4.B73 2007
891.8′687—dc22
                                                    2006032791

Typeset and designed by SAP, Brighton & Eastbourne
Printed by TJ International, Padstow, Cornwall
This book is printed on acid-free paper.

# CONTENTS

# Contents

# PREFACE

This modest publication came about from my extensive study of Czech literature, reviewing Czech books in learned periodicals, and life-time reading. When I first came to Britain in 1953 as a refugee, without any possessions, I realized that I might never see my nearest and dearest again; I also felt the separation from the culture of my nation acutely. The Iron Curtain divided Europe into two parts which did not have much to say to one another; as a refugee, one of the obvious enemies of the communist régime, I could not endanger my relatives at home by trying to contact them.

I knew that, among the masses of useless political writings, good books were being written and published in Prague. As soon as the political climate there mellowed in the sixties, my late brother (a writer and scholar in literature) as well as a few friends courageously started supplying me with books. Later, exile publishers helped to fill the gaps in my book collection, so that I was able to see the two faces of Czech literature – one suppressed at home, the other, published in exile and free.

When selecting books for this publication, I had in mind – apart from the quality of the material – the English-speaking world, what could appeal and be close enough to their way of thinking; unavoidably, this survey is not inclusive. I very much regret that so little has been translated into English so far – but hope that the present work will serve as a guide to potential translators in the future, as well as to readers.

# ACKNOWLEDGMENTS

In the first place I wish to thank Professor William Riggan, now a retired editor of *World Literature Today* (University of Oklahoma Press), for his very pleasant acceptance of my contributions to the quarterly, as well as his consent that my book reviews could be reprinted if I wished to do so. I have used a selection of them here, although not always exactly reproduced, as some have been adjusted to the format of this publication. In his last letter, his good wishes to me for arranging the publication of a volume of Czech prose writers are appreciated.

My sincere thanks also to the Academic architect Jiří Jirásek from Prague, for his kind permission to reprint his sketches: on the front of the jacket, and on pages ii, ix and 157, Jiří Jirásek, *Unás* (Prager Chronik), (trans. At Our Home – Prague Chronicle), published by Evropský Kulturní Klub-Česká Expedice (1992); and on the back of the jacket, Jiří Jirásek, in Jaromír Hořec and Ivan Janousek (eds), *Občanské Fóry* (Citizens' Jokes) published by Odeon (1990).

I am very grateful to Miss Judith Butcher of Cambridge who has read the text and corrected my English most efficiently and expertly. Dr. Ladislava Hájková from Prague supplied some biographical dates for this book, in spite of difficult circumstances in which she just then found herself; her contribution is much appreciated. My sincere thanks are due to Ing. Roman Mervart, who has been my very patient teacher and rescuer from tricky situations in which my computer occasionally trapped me. Many thanks also to Miss Vanda Procházková for her generous help in finding dates on the internet for me.

Last but not least, and once again, I wish to express my sincere gratitude to Anita Grahame, Marketing Director at Sussex Academic Press, for her admirable efficiency and expertise in enabling publication of this volume.

The hopes for freedom which were shattered by the Soviet-led invasion
From Jiří Jirásek, *Unás* (Prager Chronik)

*To the members of my former Czech Literature class at the University of the Third Age in Cambridge, who have studied with interest numerous books discussed in this volume.*

# INTRODUCTION

In Czech history, writers have been considered as spokespersons on behalf of the nation; in the last sixty years they had to struggle almost incessantly for freedom of expression and its general benefit for the life of the homeland. Munich smothered the momentous artistic growth of Masaryk's Republic; although the spirit of the arts and cultural life in general was maintained for a while afterwards, as soon as Hitler occupied the country many writers were gradually silenced, imprisoned, even exterminated in concentration camps; those who tried to write were strictly limited in their choice of subjects. The best books had to be removed from public libraries and destroyed. To avoid the same fate for private collections, their owners had to find suitable hideouts for their books, to be read and lent to friends secretly and with great caution, for punishment for keeping them was severe. Not only books of Czech liberal authors were doomed to be destroyed, the order included classics of English, American, French and Russian masters, so that only translations from Scandinavian literature could be published; they were widely read, for they represented the only cultural link of the occupied country with the outside world.

Many Czech writers kept silent, perhaps filling their drawers with writings to be published after the war (people could hardly believe in Hitler's victory), but some took to editing anthologies of poems, short stories or essays with related subjects where censorship could not deny publication. Themes from history seemed "inoffensive" and gave rise to the production of a comparatively new genre, the *biographie romancée,* the fictional biography: lives of famous painters, writers, composers (Josef Mánes, Vincent van Gogh, Francesco Goya, Paul Gauguin, Michelangelo; Louis de

Camões, Jan Neruda; Leoš Janáček – by Marie Tilschová, Vladimír Drnák, Karel Schulz, František Kožík, Soňa Špálová) could be published and became very popular. After the liberation in 1945 one could see great gaps among the writers, the victims of the Nazis; those who had survived opened their drawers containing the harvest from the war years. Authors who were popular before the war reappeared in print; new names emerged. Unfortunately, the days of freedom were numbered: after the communist *coup d'état* in 1948, the number of publishing authors shrank considerably again. Some members of the pre-war generation, like Ivan Olbracht or Josef Kopta, reached the end of their careers as writers; others had not yet recovered from the long gap of their silence during the war, or others were put off by the prospect of new censorship; those left were mainly writers who either welcomed the communist régime or found it easy to conform.

In the years of the communist rule that followed, writers had a difficult choice whether or not to join the party. As they gradually learnt to know the true face of the communist dictatorship, the enthusiasm of the idealists waned; optimists believing in some future improvement of the situation may have joined because party membership could be a hideout from police supervision and harassment, as well as a – rather dubious – chance to publish. As several cases in this publication show, there was a certain amount of fluctuation in the writers' attitude to the party membership: whether they tried to show willing or get advantages, they could be expelled from the party and accepted back (or not) after a time (like Bohumil Hrabal). Sometimes expulsion created a situation worse than the original non-membership.

The horrors of the war provided an important source of inspiration, and not only in fiction: a good number of reports came out which aimed at the registration of war events and the documentary value of which was often greater than their artistic merit. The choice of war motifs in fiction seems to have been a natural reaction to the atrocities of the war on the one hand, and on the other it was an escape into the past about which one could write with impunity. The motifs may also have been a substitute for the necessary inspiration which the spiritual and artistic sterility of the period could not provide. Conforming literary critics established the code for literary creations according to the Soviet theoretician A. A. Ždanov. Eulogies on Stalin appeared in print; non-conformists could not publish and some were even harassed. As loyalty to the communist party was a more important criterion for the valuation of a piece of writing than its art, literature lost its cream of writers, some previous idealist communists among them. Who would like to read dull stories about black-and-white characters where the white ones condemn the black ones and try to persuade "the neutrals" that a stakchanovite production in the factory or on the farm leads to the best of all worlds? The taste of Czech readers could not be satisfied by such inferior works and they turned to old classics which were reprinted in quantities, though only those officially approved of. Absurdly enough, censorship did *not* exist by law, but anything to be published had to bear the stamp of the "Principal Management of Press Supervision".

However, already in 1952 the green light for some political relaxation in literature came from the Soviet Union, in the form of Sergej Nikol'skij's slender publication on Karel Čapek who was blacklisted after 1948 again; it encouraged Čapek's Czech admirers to remind the authorities that he was too great a writer to be ignored. The difficulty lay in interpretation: bound by the rules of social realism, Czech scholars could hardly interpret Čapek freely as he deserved. Certain works of his still could not be mentioned, others had to be "re-evalued" to be accepted by the communist way of thinking. Yet, already in 1953 his posthumous fragment of *Obrázky z domova* ("Pictures from Home") came out and the state publishing house, Československý spisovatel, launched the publication of Čapek's collected works (completed in 1995). Čapek's friend František Langer (still alive then) also could publish again: his *Pražské legendy* ("Prague Legends") came out in 1956, the charming memoir *Byli a bylo* ("They Were and it Was") in 1963, *Filatelistické povídky* ("Philatelic Tales") in 1964, *Malířské povídky* ("Painters' Stories") in 1966 and *Snílci a vrahové* ("Dreamers and Murderers") in 1967.

In 1956 Khrushchev's debunking of the Stalin myth gave new hope. Some works of liberal writers appeared in print and the communist propaganda was no longer essential in the prose works. The cornerstone, however, seems to have been Škvorecký's "The

Cowards": written in 1948, it was published as late as ten years afterwards – and still created a certain amount of controversy: not only was there an individual, subjective hero, uninhibited and using colloquial language, unlike socialist-realist characters who always spoke standard Czech, but a hero who so obviously preferred members of the western liberating army to the Soviet ones! Yet, the word "democracy" was heard occasionally in speeches at communist party gatherings and writers could at least experiment with how far the term could be implied: the censor often overlooked the hidden meaning which the reader – now trained in reading between the lines – would understand.

Another spring swallow signalling new hope was the Kafka international conference in 1963, instigated by Professor Eduard Goldstücker. While some contemporary readers might have experienced frightening scenes in their daily life, comparable to those of Kafka's obscure world, his writings then represented the domain of the bourgeois decadence and were blacklisted for a number of years. Yet, Kafka was known and valued abroad – could a "re-evaluation" bring him home? Controversies about the interpretation of his work were bound to arise, but, generally, the conference meant a step forward, nevertheless.

At that stage there was no shortage of controversies between the writers and "the management"; but, at least, the writers had some voice – even if a speech too free or a book politically too critical of the régime may have resulted in the author's punishment, dismissal from the party, harassment, even prison. Škvorecký's "The Cowards" was widely read, but the possibility of its reprinting met with official hesitation. This book soon got some indirect backing by the publication of two novels, Milan Kundera's "The Joke", with its "fallacious" political undertones and the regret that a human being is not free to choose his/her own fate, and by Ludvík Vaculík's "The Axe", with its vision of the finally vain effort to create a communist dreamland. Hrabal experimented, too; sometimes he was successful with a publication, other times he failed; the Oscar-winning film version of his "Closely Observed Trains" in 1967 (ridiculing the Nazis, therefore politically not objectionable) confirmed his place among the leading writers. In the same year, as an overture to the regenerating Prague Spring, the writers at their

Union's conference turned directly against the leadership and achieved some success, although, before long, several of the protesters were expelled from the party, Klíma and Vaculík among them.

The Prague Spring, 1968, under Dubček's leadership, gave great hope for the strengthening of democracy; if only it had survived! The Warsaw Pact invasion ruthlessly wrecked all efforts leading to liberalization. Who could now claim with impunity that censorship did not exist? It took some time after Dubček's dismissal to tighten the fetters: during the next almost two years passport holders could still travel abroad (where thousands of them stayed in exile) and a few books just being printed, like Škvorecký's *Lvíče* ("Miss Silver's Past") came out – only to appear on the black list soon afterwards. The writers in their Union tried hard to defend their right to write freely; literary journals abounded in controversies which, before long, led to the closure of most of them. In 1970 a new list of banned books was issued and purges of library books were renewed, after the wartime fashion. The Writers' Union was disbanded in 1972, to be replaced by a new one; names of the best writers did not appear on the list of members and an opportunity for promotion of the second-rate thus arose. The few remaining gifted authors could not save the situation; they, too, had to return to neutral subjects from history or the war (Ladislav Fuks) or the dreary present (Vladimír Páral). The established "normalization" threatened like the sword of Damocles.

Once again Czech literature found itself in a straitjacket. It was not for the first time in history that Czech books were printed abroad and smuggled into the country, even at the price of the carrier's being severely punished if caught. The persecution of the Czech Brethren after the Battle of the White Mountain, 1620, comes to mind as an example; the illegal import could be tried again. Exiled writers abroad could express themselves freely, but other factors hindered them from creating their best. There were only a few professional writers among the first-phase exiles (1948–68), Egon Hostovský, Jan Čep, Zdeněk Němeček among them. But their numbers increased considerably after the Warsaw Pact invasion of Czechoslovakia, 1968. They found themselves practically penniless (their "home" currency not being convertible for individuals in western countries) among sympathetic people speaking a different language (but, no, Boris Pasternak was not quite right in his belief that a creative writer can write well only in his native country – the Czech situation eventually proved the contrary!): their expression in their first language was bound to be influenced, in the negative sense more likely than in the positive. Whether a professional or a young budding author, they found themselves initially involved in economic problems when establishing the basis of their living from scratch, perhaps even spending their energy, for a time, as "cheap foreign labourers". In the absence of sponsors or benefactors abroad, what chance was there to find a publisher for a book in Czech? And who would read it? There must have been then lots of feelings of isolation among Czech exile writers – not, perhaps, as the most damaging factor, for, if they resented communism while in their home country, they could have felt isolated already there just the same; but, more importantly, they found themselves separated, perhaps for ever, from their families who stayed at home, as any communication with them would lead to their persecution by the régime.

Yet, the spirit of the free Czech literature survived with the exiles' help. While the early refugees managed to establish several periodicals in western countries (*Sklizeň, Proměny, Nový život, Západ, Svědectví,* to name a few) exiles after 1968, numbering something between 100,000 and 150,000, increased the resources very much indeed. Not only that there were more writers among them, but, gradually, several publishing houses could be instituted. "Sity-Eight Publishers" in Toronto, owned by Zdena and Josef Škvorecký, remains the most important, although, also in 1972, the "Index" in Cologne was opened. "Konfrontace" appeared in Zurich, "Rozmluvy" in London, "Arkýř" in Munich where also one of the earliest, CCC Books, connected with the Radio Free Europe, was founded; "Křesťanská akademie" in Rome specialized in religious literature. As the Czech readers were dispersed over much of the free world, the publishers had to use a kind of mail order system; they worked very hard and struggled with financial problems, but their enthusiasm outweighed material losses. The most important cultural institution, the Czechoslovak Society of Arts and Sciences in America (Společnost pro vědy a uměni), founded in the late fifties, flourished in playing its part very efficiently.

So, once again, Czech books were smuggled – now to the communist Czechoslovakia, with great risks both for the transporters and the eager receivers. In the meantime, in the homeland blacklisted writers learnt how to communicate with their readers by way of irony, satire, allegory, black humour to camouflage what they *really* wished to say; as their works were often refused publication, they invented their self-help in the form of *samizdat* (edice Petlice, Expedice . . . ) – books being typed and produced at home in the Do-it-Yourself way and secretly distributed among people of like minds. Now, at last, authors at home and abroad could cooperate: manuscripts were smuggled abroad to be published by exile publishers and then smuggled back for the Czechs at home. Owing to the régime's vigilance, it was a very dangerous game and we know only too well about the harassment the writers like Václav Havel and many others had to suffer. Their number is high, in fact, many of them are included in this book. Why did they resist so much? The régime could stop publication within the country but was powerless to do the same abroad. They harassed their victims in brutal, vindictive ways, but now had to so with caution, for the world was watching and insisting on human rights. After a long struggle, once again, the writers' voice on behalf of the nation was heard and has brought success.

# HANA BĚLOHRADSKÁ

## *Bez krásy, bez límce*
### ("Without Beauty, Without Collar")
Prague, Československý spisovatel, 1964

HANA BĚLOHRADSKÁ (1929–2005) studied law in Prague for one year, worked as a laboratory assistant at the First Children's Clinic and since 1961 has been a professional writer. As from 1970 she was not allowed to publish, so she worked on translations (Ruth Rendell among others), using a cover name for their publications. She became very active in cultural life after 1989.

Her prose works demonstrate her interest in the moral and psychological aspects of life influenced by inevitable historical circumstances. Her début, *Bez krásy, bez límce* (1962, 1964), set in the war-time atmosphere, with a suffering Jewish hero, was received very well by the critics. External circumstances causing a change in the relationship of a married couple play the main part in *Vítr se stočí k jihovýchodu* ("The Wind will Turn towards South-east", 1963). In *Poslední večeře* ("The Last Supper", 1966), from a hospital milieu, Bělohradská combined a detective theme with psychological problems of the protagonists. In 1994 her collection of short stories *Nebezpečné výpravy* ("Dangerous Excursions") came out. The euphoria of the Velvet Revolution, with some disillusions which followed, is reflected in *Titanik a jiné povídky* ("The Titanic and Other Stories"), Prague, Academia, 2004.

### *Bez krásy, bez límce*

The horrors of the Nazi occupation of Czechoslovakia have been a powerful source of inspiration for Czech writers since the liberation in 1945. Indeed, twenty years later the subject had still not faded out, as this novelette shows. Bělohradská presents here a series of events, only too familiar to those who lived in the Protectorate during the war; yet her dealing with the subject is far from hackneyed.

In her indignation about the futility of war, the inhumanity and sadism of the Nazis, the author created a pitiful central character of a Jew, Dr. Braun, once a prosperous doctor, now, aged over seventy, a ruined outcast, an innocent victim of the Nazi hatred. Driven out of his house, he is moved into a flat in a block, quite alone since his wife left him and his son managed to escape abroad. He feels that his life has lost its sense, but the kindness of the other Czech residents in the block, their sympathy and solidarity with those who are persecuted more than themselves, encourage him. He regains his spirit after he has succeeded in saving the life of a member of the underground movement from an attack of pneumonia and from the German police. Unfortunately, his Czech friends cannot save Dr. Braun from the increasing Nazi persecution. He dies, exhausted by forced, degrading hard labour, clearing the ever-accumulating snow from the Prague streets.

Apart from Dr. Braun there is a variety of other characters. Each person and family is affected by the occupation in a different way; these comparatively brief scenes, without any firm link between them (except for the silent, passive resistance to the Germans) form the core of the plot. It is just everyday life of ordinary people, life without beauty, with sharp conflicts of tension, drawn skilfully. The first chapter, introducing Dr. Braun, is particularly good because of its lucidity and brevity. The terse style and art of characterization show Bělohradská as a promising fiction writer already in this early work of hers.

# JAN BENEŠ

## *Trojúhelník s Madonou*
### ("A Triangle with Madonna")
### Toronto, Sixty-Eight Publishers, 1980

JAN BENEŠ (born 1936), son of an architect, attended the school of arts and crafts (1951–1955) and worked later in this field for a short time. He did not settle in any permanent post until he became a free-lance writer. His secret regular contributions to the exile journal *Svědectví* (Paris) earned him a five-year jail sentence in 1966, but an amnesty in 1968 shortened it to just two; in 1990 he was fully reha-bilitated. After his emigration to the United States in 1969 he again experienced a variety of occupations, including occasional lecturing about Czech literature at American universities and a study, followed by a lectureship, at the Defense Language Institute at Monterey, California. All the while he was contributing to a good number of journals, both in his own country (while there) and in exile.

Beneš's work consists mostly of short stories and not too long novels; in these genres he is quite prolific. As far as subjects are concerned, some of his characters resent the flow of time spent in banal situations, others show some kind of dissatisfaction with life wherever they live. Beneš wittily criticizes everything communist, while, on the other hand, people in the US and the rest of the free world seem to be somehow insufficiently experienced in the hard ways of life (cf. *Banánové sny,* "Banana Dreams", Zurich, Konfrontace, 1984).

Topics from prison life can be found in *Na místě* ("On the Spot", Toronto, Sixty-Eight Publishers, 1972), *Druhý dech* (Zurich,

Konfrontace, 1974, "The Second Breath", New York, 1969) and *Žádné kvítí* ("No Flowers", London, Rozmluvy, 1986). Beneš's first book, *Do vrabců jako když střelí* ("A Shot into a Flock of Sparrows"), came out as early as in 1962, to be followed in Prague by *Situace* ("A Situation", 1963) and *Disproporce* ("Disproportion", 1969); afterwards he published abroad, apart from the above-mentioned three: *Až se se mnou vyspíš… budeš plakat* ("After You Have Slept With me… You Will Cry", Köln, Index, 1973), *Zelenou nahoru* ("Green Side Up", Toronto, Sixty-Eight Publishers, 1977), and *Trojúhelník s Madonou* (1980).

Beneš returned home from the exile in 1990 and published there *Indolence* ("Indolence", 1993) and *Svoboda nechodí v rudém* ("Freedom does not Wear Red", 1995).

## *Trojúhelník s Madonou*

Graham Greene very much approved of Jan Beneš's earlier novel, "The Second Breath", saying that, although every work about labour camps necessarily stands in Solzhenitzyn's shadow, he himself preferred "The Second Breath" to *One Day in the Life of Ivan Denisovich*. Comparing *Trojúhelník s Madonou* with *Druhý dech*, it seems that the former stands in the shadow of the latter; in fact, thematically, the earlier work could almost be a sequel to *Trojúhelník s Madonou,* which culminates with the hero's sentence to a labour camp. There are also other similarities: the main characters in both suffer from restricted confinement, a labour camp and National Service respectively, and both get involved (though in different circumstances) in acts of violence, which lead to the correction cells in the former novel and to the labour camp in the latter. In both works the stuffy atmosphere is drawn powerfully, and it seems that the bullying and wanton infliction of authority on the conscripts during the Stalinist period did not differ too much from that imposed on the labour camp inmates.

However, while *The Second Breath* has no female characters and structurally follows a pattern similar to that of *Ivan Denisovich,* the main drama in *Trojúhelník s Madonou* concentrates on Private Milan, his officer Pavel and "the Madonna", Pavel's wife Olina. Conscription is taken as an inevitable evil by the young soldiers, and

Milan tries to spend as pleasantly as possible his days of confinement in a small, dull town in Slovakia where his unit is stationed. A few nights with a not very attractive waitress from the local public house provide some relief from the monotonous routine, but after an afternoon spent in a hotel with Olina, he feels that this is the kind of pleasure worth developing into a deeper relationship. However, on his way back the exuberant Milan gets into a clash with an officer and finds himself in a labour camp, without having any chance to see Olina again; the 219 days remaining to complete his National Service turn into 976 in the labour camp, a price which he pays, indirectly, for his fleeting affair with his officer's wife. Yet, he thinks that it is worthwhile – a conclusion which makes one wonder about the values these people hold, if a moment of physical pleasure can make up for the subsequent labour camp experience. This climax seems rather inconsistent with the previous implication that Milan was inclined to put Olina on a pedestal; the fact that she never has the chance to learn to know about his changed situation may perhaps indicate the "message" about human relationships in a situation where authorities exercise their power to manipulate their citizens' lives, without regard to the human element in the circumstances of the cases involved.

The novel is well written, the characters convincingly presented and the seemingly trivial plot sufficiently interspersed with moments of tension; Beneš's wit and humour produce some effectively grotesque situations. It is refreshing to see that the story is not obsessed with sex, as much of contemporary Czech prose tends to be.

# IRENA DOUSKOVÁ

## *Někdo s nožem*
("Someone with a Knife")
Prague, Hynek, 2000

IRENA DOUSKOVÁ (born 1964) was born in Prague where she later studied law. She is a free-lance writer as well as editor of *Maskil* ("The Enlightener"), a monthly journal of a small liberal Jewish congregation *Bejt Simcha* ("House of Joy"). She has developed the short story as her favourite genre (so far). *Hrdý Budžes* ("The Proud Budžes", 1998), a collection of amusing stories on the background of the deplorable period of the "normalization" in the seventies, scenes as seen by an eight-year-old girl Helenka Součková, is particularly successful and has also been performed on the stage in its dramatic form.

"The Proud Budžes" was preceded by *Goldstein píše své dceři* ("Goldstein Writes to his Daughter", 1997) and followed by *Doktor Kott přemítá* ("Doctor Kott Contemplates", 2002) – twelve short stories marked by the existentialist anxiety in the post-communist society. In 2004 further short stories came out, *Čím se liší tato noc* ("What Distinguishes this Night"); as in the previous stories, Dousková writes about ordinary people in her simple, but powerful language.

*Někdo s nožem* ("Someone with a Knife", 2000) is – so far – her only novel; albeit a slim book, but her witty, terse style is full of meaning. Dousková is a gifted observer and narrator of both external events as well as her own thoughts. The latter appear deeper than M. Viewegh's to critics (Bára Gregorová, Jan Čulík) who compare their artistic achievements. She is brave enough to use the

Prague dialect, for that is the true language of her thoughts, the most natural way of her communication with the reader.

## *Někdo s nožem*

At first glance this short novel could be described as one about a frustrated housewife, a subject so common that one wonders whether truly interesting variations on the theme can be created. Yet, the book is captivating and well written.

The form of (mostly brief) diary entries – a kind of interior monologue – lends itself well for expressing the heroine's frustration. In her honesty, she does not blame anyone for her lot; in fact, she finds excuses for other people's attitudes and behaviour. As she looks after her two young daughters, alone for long periods, she accepts the loneliness of her monotonous life as inevitable. No, she is not a single mother; she loves her decent, faithful husband who provides well for the family, but his work keeps him away a lot, and he does not have much to say when at home. Infrequently, there are communications with her divorced parents, her in-laws, a female school friend, or a former boyfriend, but they do not make her life more colourful, so that her normal day looks like this: "Nobody phoned, I didn't phone anybody, nobody called. Afternoon, usual stroll in the fen. Short dusk, quick darkness. A long one, of course. But Candlemas not far away."

Yet, dull as her life may be, the heroine observes keenly all that is going on around her in the neighbourhood, meditating and commenting wittily and poignantly. The reader is not left in doubt that she loves her family, parents and in-laws, even if she is shy to show it and is often puzzled or amused, as the case may be, by their individual oddities. But what about the title "Someone with a Knife"? The heroine's long periods on her own (while the children sleep) bring about her insomnia and anxiety that some dangerous individual might be lurking in the flat. This experience creates tension in the novel, but does not seem to signal the final tragedy yet. Neither does her father's obsession with the security of his new house and his purchase of an additional revolver. She may laugh at his whim, but it is this weapon in her father's hands which kills her accidentally when she visits him unexpectedly, at an unusual hour.

The tragedy happens suddenly and is devastating, just at a time when the prospects for the heroine's life were beginning to look brighter.

Since the heroine cannot enter her own death in the diary, the author uses for this purpose a frame of italicized passages written by the heroine's husband in reaction to reading her diary; his interior monologue provides the disentanglement, adding some extra touches to the picture as well. A few characters contribute in a similar way to fill information for the reader.

It may sound paradoxical, but this slender novel about a dull life is fresh, penetrating, witty and credible.

# VIKTOR FISCHL

## *Kafka v Jerusalému*
("Kafka in Jerusalem")
Prague, Český spisovatel, 1996

## *Maškary v Benátkách*
("Masks in Venice")
Prague, Primus, 1997

VIKTOR FISCHL, born in 1912 to a Czech Jewish family in Hradec Králové, Bohemia (then part of the Austro-Hungarian monarchy), studied law and sociology in Prague and spent most of his working life in the diplomatic service. As soon as Hitler's army occupied his homeland in 1939, he emigrated to London where he worked at the Foreign Office of the Czechoslovak exile government between 1940 and 1944. Here he became close to Jan Masaryk (cf. *Hovory s Janem Masarykem*, "Conversations with Jan Masaryk", Tel Aviv, 1951). He served the liberated Czechoslovakia from 1945 till 1949 in London and Prague, but left in 1949 for Israel, whom he represented as ambassador in several countries.

He wrote poetry first. In 1951 his prose *Píseň o lítosti* ("A Song about Sorrow") came out, but he turned to prose writing again after a fairly long interval. Thanks to his imagination and his pure heart, he developed a gentle, lyrical, witty style to express simple human actions in beautiful terms. In *Kuropění* ("Cockcrow before Dawn", Zurich, Konfrontace, 1975) a lonely village doctor finds – after some upsets in his life – beauty and happiness in his decision to serve the village people, having been inspired by the company of and "discussions" with his beautiful, indomitable pet cock. *Hrací hodiny* ("A Musical Clock", Zurich, Polygon, 1982) impresses the readers' minds by the clock which belonged to the same family for generations and which played a minuet every hour; a ritual devolved from this, that, as long as they were in, the father gave a kiss to his wife every hour, no matter how otherwise occupied he might have been; sometimes the couple also danced. A collection of charming short stories, *Jeruzalémské povídky* ("Jerusalem Stories") came out in 1985, to be followed by the novel *Dvorní šašci* ("The Court Clowns", 1990), published, like the rest of Fischl's books, in Prague: *Kafka v Jeruzalému*,1996, *Maškary v Benátkách*, 1997, *Loučení s Jeruzalémem* ("Farewell to Jerusalem", 1997) and *Hovory s jabloní* ("Talks with an Apple Tree", 1999). In the last one, the apple tree has a similar function to that of the pet cock in *Kuropění*: for the lonely hero's meditations (he is a joiner this time) it is a symbol of stability, beauty, sweetness and fertility. His most recent *Vy soudci athénští* ("You Judges of Athens") came out in 2005.

In all his novels Fischl has kept up the values which J. Dresler had already appreciated in the afterword to *Kuropění*: "Fischl remains faithful to the traditional qualities in Czech literature, such as manliness, nobility, sense of proportion, restrained elegance of expression, appreciation of the virtue of honest work, general awareness of the limits and potential of the language and, above all, the shy beauty which does not need to use glaring images, hysterical emotions and a language of the street in order to express our world."

## *Kafka v Jeruzalému*

"Jerusalem isn't like other towns, therefore people living there are also different," says the author in the introduction, and he repeats the same statement as he concludes the collection. It is certainly true about his characters in these charming tales; himself a citizen of Jerusalem as well, Fischl appears here as a raconteur who can turn everyday events into great stories.

The author is an admirer of Kafka, who figures in the opening and closing tales. On a train, as the narrator slumbers, his co-traveller takes the shape of Kafka himself; his luggage label shows the name Josef K. This visionary Kafka is met by two friends, Max and Felix (like the real Kafka's close friends Max Brod and Felix Weltsch), then disappears, only to turn up later at the Wailing Wall, pushing a slip of paper into it and vanishing into the wall himself, not like a beetle, but rather as an ant. The search for him in this Kafkaesque world ends in a most efficient Lost Property Office, by which time the mystery recedes to make room for scenes of sheer hilarity. Anything is possible in a dream, but the narrator's sunstroke in the final story also evokes dreamlike visions of Kafka's world.

Moving to more realistic looks at life in Jerusalem, we meet such common characters as a tailor, a glazier, a barber, a postman, a café owner, and the flautist of a police band. There are touching situations, as parents support one another in grief after having lost children through disease or misadventure. Two deformed victims of Nazi medical experiments make the best of their lives among sympathetic people. It is even possible for a Jew to make friends with an Arab, as they follow with interest the life of an adopted foundling whom they have saved from abandonment; a hint of rivalry is felt as they wonder about his parentage, but the promising boy shocks them by becoming a terrorist, stabbing his Jewish rescuer and getting himself shot by an approaching patrol.

Fischl sees the more humorous aspects of a madman's antics, but at the same time he draws a pathetic portrait of a former stationmaster in Terezín who was forced to transport thousands of his own people to their deaths, himself going mad as a result. A barber takes on himself the collective guilt for not having changed the course of history: could not those who shaved Hitler, Musolini, Eichmann and Stalin have tilted the razor slightly and slit their throats? A tailor, prosperous in spite of all odds, has had his share of family misfortunes, but feels happy again when both his account number and the name of his Swiss bank vanish from his memory. The mysterious word *mucharem* rouses curiosity about this special date when both landlords and tenants are freed from their contracts and a good many change residence; as they transport their humble possessions on carts or on their own backs, a bed in the street bearing two academics discussing Spinoza may not be an unusual sight.

Since the residents of Jerusalem come from all parts of the world, their experiences are like a colourful carpet; the effects of the Holocaust still linger in the background, but Fischl's humanity makes his characters tolerant and cooperative. "Kafka in Jerusalem" is only a slim book, but it contains much wisdom, a good deal of sympathy and plenty of good-natured humour.

## Maškary v Benátkách

This book has something in common with Karel Čapek's satirical *War with the Newts.* Apart from the journalistic streak in both works, the authors also share an admiration for the great progress in science, while questioning its lasting benefits and contribution to real human happiness. Čapek has invented his science-fiction newts as the centre of his speculation, and Fischl's Doctor Faustus and Mephisto put on their masks; both writers skilfully spin their stories, making the reader believe the unbelievable, but the writers do so with a great deal of imagination, wit and charm.

The scene is Venice, more precisely the Umbertino Palace, now owned and recently restored by a rich Japanese businessman, where a splendid fancy-dress ball, to which the world's celebrities are invited, is held to celebrate the "take-over". Mephisto, keeping his promise to allow Faust a short spell of time on earth each century, is more generous on this occasion, as the millennium is approaching: thus, the necessary span of time for the development of the plot is gained.

Uninformed for the whole century about the state of affairs in the world, Faust has to have many puzzling things explained to him: for example, why Albert Einstein is doomed to three days a week in hell (for contributing to the birth of the atom bomb), while the remaining four he can enjoy in heaven, playing second violin, with Haydn playing the first, Rabindranath Tagore the cello, and Saint Cecilia the viola (his merits being greater than his sins). Faust acknowledges with a certain amount of satisfaction the fact that the common language in hell in this century is German, though a substantial minority of Russians claim their share.

Tongue in cheek, the author tries to assure us that any similarity between his characters and actual individual persons is purely coincidental, but, under their masks, individuals reminiscent of public figures from all walks of life appear on the scene. It would require a good deal of ignorance, should Salman Rushdie pass unrecognized in Fischl's Bahram Abhazi. His case provides tension and eventual disentanglement of the plot which the author solves with a skill appropriate to his former profession as a diplomat, just as he wittily preserves the veracity of other characters once they begin to approach the brink of disbelief. Actually, the recipe of faked murder and assumption of a new identity may not be quite so simple for the real Salman Rushdie, but it lends itself well to the expression of Fischl's anguish about the changing values in our society; in this century of intolerance and violence, love resulting in progeny can be replaced by an injection needle, the meaning of love and adultery have merged, and the bed appears to be the site of ultimate bliss.

Fischl's Abhasi, with a new identity and removed from the lime-light of publicity, still has a good chance to write, but finds satisfaction in ordinary employment and in the true love of his unpretentious, charming wife and family. The tip on the scale on which Fischl compares his ideas about life on earth and in his imaginary hell inclines considerably toward the latter. He is neither gloomy nor didactic, however, but rather the contrary: he, too, like K. Čapek, can make the reader think while laughing.

# LADISLAV FUKS

## *Variace pro temnou strunu*
## ("Variations for a Dark String")
Prague, Československý spisovatel, 1966

LADISLAV FUKS' (1923–1994) father was a police officer. He studied philosophy, psychology, history of art and education at the university in Prague (Ph.D. 1949), worked for a few years in the paper industry and later as a specialist in the State Institute for the Care of Old Monuments and the National Gallery, respectively, until he became a professional writer. The number of periodicals to which he contributed included two Jewish journals, *"Židovský věstník* ("Jewish Bulletin") and *Židovská ročenka* ("Jewish Yearbook").

He started writing and publishing fiction in the sixties when wartime Jewish themes flourished in contemporary literature; his characters, often alienated and anxious, seem to live in an atmosphere of fear, crime and horror, as if a catastrophe were imminent. And of course catastrophe does come eventually, in the shape of Hitler and all that followed in this connection.

The Jewish hero of his first novel, *Pan Theodor Mundstock* ("Mr. Theodore Mundstock", 1963), visualizes various ways in which he could possibly survive the Nazi death transport, but, paradoxically, is killed by a German car. The collection of short stories *Mí černovlasí bratři* ("My Dark-haired Brothers", 1964) and the novel *Variace pro temnou strunu* ("Variations for a Dark String", 1966) take the reader into the world of adolescent Jewish boys; the novel *Spalovač mrtvol* ("The Cremator" 1967) shows a weird protagonist whose mind, crippled by the experience of war, leads him to act as a criminal. *Myši Natalie Mooshabrové* ("The Mice of Natalie

Mooshaber", 1970) could be described as a fantastic horror story, while *Příběh kriminálního rady* ("The Story of a Police Commissioner", 1971) deals with a case of detection.

In *Nebožtíci na bále* ("The Dead Taking Part in a Ball", 1972) Fuks returned for inspiration to the past and his "dark-haired brothers"; he drew a picture of life in a Slovak village, transformed after the war, in *Pasáček z doliny* ("A Little Shepherd from the Valley", 1973). Dealing with the subject of exiles from the communist régime in *Návrat z žitného pole* ("Return from a Wheatfield", 1974) Fuks takes the official line; and he looks back to war again in *Obraz Martina Blaskowitze* ("The Picture of Martin Blaskowitz", 1980). Fuks' art of narration culminates in his masterpiece, *Vévodkyně a kuchařka* ("The Duchess and the Cook", 1983), presenting the contrasting destinies of the two main characters on the historical background of life in Vienna at the turn of the 19th and 20th centuries.

### *Variace pro temnou strunu*

This novel is an interesting psychological study of a boy in his early teens, living in Prague just before the last war. Although he is the only son of a high-ranking well-to-do police officer, his childhood is anything but happy; in fact, Fuks's protagonist grows up almost alienated from his own parents, unable to develop any human emotional ties, because there is no one to help him in this respect. His material comfort is guaranteed, but when it comes to little problems that worry or puzzle him, the only refuge he feels he can take is in the portrait of his grandmother in a lonely room; to this lifeless object young Michal keeps coming to confide. The maid servant Růženka and his schoolmates provide some sort of company for him, but none of them is near enough to him. The child remains spiritually isolated in the society in which he lives.

The father's frequent absence from home and a certain ambiguity about his profession, unknown visitors and people who seem to keep watch over the house, suggest some intriguing mystery about the place; the child's imagination and intuition create this sort of atmosphere, and it is through him that the writer communicates with the reader. The unknown, the unexplained leads to some kind of subconscious fear in the child's mind who perceives the world at first through fairy-tale images; as he grows, the boyish sense of the adventurous interprets situations differently, until reality shows its proper face: it is a sad, disturbing reality, for Austria and the Sudetenland have been occupied by the Nazis and the world is preparing for war. Michal is too young to understand fully all the political events, but his subconscious anxiety and fears, the dark string in his soul, create the image of a murderer walking by; consequently, his reactions to things he perceives even anticipate for the reader some horrors which the subsequent war inflicted on Michal's nation; for instance, the father's book containing pictures of murdered people suggests to the reader the scenes in the concentration camps; the janitor's red gown with a pointed hood and an axe hidden in a cupboard bring an executioner to the reader's mind; furnaces in a factory symbolize camp crematoria.

The book is full of tension, as the author makes Michal as well as other characters speculate about various events or their potential consequences for their own uncertain future. The maid Růženka and her female friend, a greengrocer, get very excited (and the reader is made curious) by the fortune-teller's prediction that the greengrocer will marry a general; at the peak of the suspense Fuks changes the scene suddenly, only to wind off this and similar loose ends eventually, by the greengrocer's wedding to an officer of the Salvation Army. But amusing moments of this kind are rare, the book being brightened, apart from Michal's childish misinterpretations of what he sees around him, by the pranks of the schoolboys and the Czech lessons of their eccentric teacher. Otherwise, the book is gloomy, including the boys' visit to the cemetery at Hallowe'en, in its *memento mori* atmosphere. In the background there are hints about the death of T. G. Masaryk, the disturbances in the Sudetenland, Runciman's visit, the September mobilization, the Munich agreement and eventually the country's occupation in March 1939. The mysterious man whom Michal meets by chance in a park at the beginning of the novel, appears again towards the end, in a touching scene which leaves a deep impression on Michal: the man was an orchestral conductor, presumably Jewish, who was hoping to find a new home in the free pre-war Czechoslovakia, but must now leave before it is too late: "When I went to school, it would not occur to me that I might ever lose my home. That I shall have to leave it and, no sooner do I settle down in another country, that I would have to go on . . . Man is an eternal refugee and fugitive. To lose one's home is the worst thing" (p. 309).

Symbolism is one of Fuks' frequent technical devices; Michal's sensitivity, imagination and visions actually necessitate this. The colour (sometimes connected with superstition which characterizes the simplicity of Růženka and her chums) is quite effective in this novel, but some symbols may lead to different interpretations of the same text, creating a disturbing ambiguity. Is Fuks trying to persuade us in one of the last passages that – since they both wear a high-ranking officer's uniform – there is really not much difference between Michal's father and the officer who has brought an SS man to search Michal's home ruthlessly? Or, why should the janitor Hron, who curses the Nazi intruders, be associated with the SS man whose canine teeth and bloodshed eyes suggest a wolf? Are we to take it that the plurality created by the vibration of "the dark string" is similar to the plurality Karel Čapek expresses through his hero of *An Ordinary Life*, representing in one man the potential qualities of many? However, Fuks' meditation over the term "seelenlos" (soulless), used in German and attributed to the SS man as well as the ghost in a Czech ballad (which the author mentions several times), suggest rather the writer's worry about the decline of humanity – lack of kindness and sympathy toward one another, the *homo homini lupus* attitude symbolized by the SS man.

The novel is likely to make its readers think; its gloomy subject may depress some and the ambiguity of the last part may even puzzle them.

In English

*Mr. Theodore Mundstock*, Iris Urwin, trans., New York, Orion Press, 1968.
  New York, Four Walls Eight Windows, 1991.
*The Cremator*, Eva Kandler, trans., London, New York, Marion Boyars, 1984.

# VÁCLAV HAVEL

## Do různých stran
("In Various Directions")

Vilém Prečan, ed., Prague, *Lidové noviny*, 1990

VÁCLAV HAVEL (born 1936), now retired as President of the Czech Republic, may be known mainly for his remarkable political achievements, but he has been also an important figure in the literary world, as a dramatist and essayist. He came from a prominent family: his father, his paternal grandfather and his uncle Miloš have left distinctive hallmarks on Prague cultural life by their great enterprise as building-contracting engineers; the maternal grandfather as well as Václav's father brought the art of writing into the family by their book publications; all of them had varied, successful careers. While Václav received a first-class primary education, he was caught by the last war and the communist régime, which adversely influenced his formal higher education. Only in 1966, after some experience as a theatre technician and assistant producer, did he finish his study at the University Faculty of Drama. He made a name for himself as an innovative dramatist, but his political activities, with his brave stand against communism, which resulted in several terms of imprisonment but led eventually to his Presidency, made him even more renowned, loved and respected.

As far as prose is concerned, Havel produced innumerable essays, published at first either in *samizdat* editions (like the Expedice) in Prague or abroad, to be freely reprinted in Prague after the fall of communism. Only a few collections can be mentioned here: *O lidskou identitu* ("On Human Identity", London, 1984), *Dálkový výslech* ("A Long-Distance Interview", Prague, Expedice, 1986),

*Living in Truth* (for which he was awarded the Erasmus Prize and which also contains the stoical essay "The Power of the Powerless", Amsterdam/London, 1986), and *Do různých stran*, 1990. Shortly before he became President, he wrote *Letní přemítání* ("Summer Meditations", Prague, Odeon, 1991).

Although Havel experienced only a few years of life in the first Czechoslovak Republic, he was brought up in the spirit of T. G. Masaryk's ideas of democracy and complete integrity. No wonder that his election as President of the state meant also the nation's hope for the renewal of the pre-war spirit. Presidential duties and, later, health problems have taken Havel away from writing – even if, no doubt, he still has a lot to say.

## Do různých stran

With the renewal of democracy in Czechoslovakia the popular traditional newspaper *Lidové noviny* could be printed again and it is no wonder that in its book publishing section Havel's *Do různých stran* was chosen for their first publication. It is a substantial collection of prose writings from the years 1983–89, when Havel still felt very insecure about both his country's future as well as his own. His preceding works, "On Human Identity", "Letters to Olga" and "A Long-Distance Interview" have already given the readers more than a glimpse into his life, his way of thinking and his uncompromising fight for truth and justice; this volume offers even deeper insights into his profoundly moral attitudes, the humanitarian concept of his philosophy, and his courage in resisting the evils of prevarication, indifference and the state's exploitation of its own citizens.

As the title suggests, Havel speaks here "in many directions", addressing a broad audience on a variety of subjects grouped into seven categories: dialogues; essays and articles; notes on culture and politics; introductions, afterwords, memoirs and obituaries; theatre; letters, declarations and protests; public speeches. Addenda include six items from the years 1965–83, defending writers' freedom of expression and citing the important role of the Writers' Union in 1968, plus a 1968 letter to Alexander Dubček, and two letters from prison. The three essays "Politics and Conscience", "Anatomy of Reticence" and "Thriller" perhaps explain best the new President's political and philosophical concepts, but even in the earlier writings one can see his tremendous concern at the suffocating atmosphere of the communist régime and his unceasing efforts to effect changes so that his nation's dormant positive values might be reawakened.

Havel's writing is clear and exact, his thinking cool and unaffected by the continual stress and tension of the mid-eighties; his often poetic images add poignancy to his words. His life under constant police surveillance during those years resembled a dance among eggs, but he never lost faith: "What can we do? Not worry about ideological pseudoproblems but try – now, here, always and everywhere – to bring about a change for the better, to obtain greater freedom and more respect for human dignity, to improve the economy, to do less harm to the atmosphere, to wish for a government of more sensible politicians so that one might speak the truth" ("Farce, Reformability, and the Future of the World").

The editor V. Prečan deserves special praise for his truly professional and conscientious work. The publication is fully annotated and contains a chronology, a complete bibliography and an essay by E. Kriseová on Havel's life and work. All this makes it easy to find one's way, so that the author can truly be heard speaking "in various directions".

In English

*On Human Identity*, London, 1984.
*The Anatomy of Reticence*, Stockholm, Charter 77 Foundation, 1986.
*Living in Truth*, London, Faber and Faber, 1989.
*Disturbing the Peace (Dálkový výslech)*, Paul Wilson, trans., London, Faber and Faber, 1990.
*Letters to Olga*, Paul Wilson, trans., London, Faber and Faber, 1990.
*Open Letters:* Selected Prose. Paul Wilson, trans., London, Faber and Faber, 1991.
*Summer Meditations*, Paul Wilson, trans., London, Faber and Faber, 1992.
*The Art of the Impossible* (Speeches and Writings 1990–1996), Paul Wilson and others, trans., New York, Knopf, 1997.

# MILOSLAVA HOLUBOVÁ

## *Víc než jeden život*
Prague, Melantrich, 1994

## "More than One Life"
Translated by Alex Zucker, Lyn Coffin, and Zdenka Brodská
(Evanston, Ill., Northwestern University Press, 1999)

MILOSLAVA HOLUBOVÁ (born 1913) was educated at the classics-orientated grammar school in Brno. She then studied law, but found more interest in the history of art and classical archaeology. These studies at the Charles University at Prague were interrupted in the fifties by her imprisonment for her membership among the dissidents. In the seventies she was brave enough to sign the Charter 77 and enjoyed an affectionate, close friendship with the philosopher Professor Jan Patočka, one of the most important leaders of the dissidents.

She became professor of history of art at the arts and crafts academy in Prague and lectured there between 1954 and 1973. Apart from essays, she published short stories, *Filatelista* ("A Stamp Collector", 1958) and *Už zase krmím holuby na náměstí* ("Again I Feed Pigeons on the Square", 1978). Her elegant, poetical style and cultivated, impartial mind characterize her two main, memoir-type, publications, *Víc než jeden život* ("More than One Life", 1994; the first edition was entitled *Posmrtný život*, "Posthumous Life") and *Necestou cestou* ("Off the Beaten Track", 1998), the latter dealing with the life of a family in the background of events in the 20th century, and including pen portraits of prominent personalities of Czech cultural and spiritual life. Among them there is a touching story of Věra Hrůzová, Karel Čapek's love and inspiration for his novel *Krakatit* and, most prominently, the author's relationship with Jan Patočka.

## Víc než jeden život

Can a writer squeeze "more than one life" (as the title claims) into a slim volume like this, Holubová's first work to be translated into English? The whole family takes part, so their stories might provide enough material for an extensive chronicle; but *More than One Life* was hardly meant to be a full-size novel. It reads like a memoir, narrated by one of the daughters of the family involved, and is likely to include autobiographical traits. As an art historian and the author of numerous essays in that field, as well as poetry, the author adopts a lyrical tone here. Having reached the mature age when one looks back to one's past with nostalgia and without prejudice, she sets the characters in Czechoslovakia as far back as the 1930s onward.

This was a turbulent period in the country's history. Holubová herself lived through the war and experienced imprisonment under the communists, and she also took part in the liberal Charter 77 movement, but she touches upon political background events only casually, her interest being focused on the main protagonist, the father of the family, a chemical engineer like Holubová's own father. In him she creates a fine portrait of a man whom all suppose to be happy, yet who was made shy and insecure by various circumstances and conventions. He misunderstands his sensitive wife, and, as his increasing disorientation and growing sense of feeling rejected and unloved make him more and more irritable and depressed, his children gradually become alienated from him. Isolated, he ultimately leaves his family and even attempts suicide, only to find much later the fulfilment of his craving for affection in the genuine love shown by his grandson.

After the mother has been removed from the scene by early death, the four siblings, including the narrator, seek someone to relate to (hence perhaps "more than one life?"). The author uses a kind of two-way narration, simultaneously directed toward the reader on the one hand, and communicating on the other with people like the elderly gentleman who, a stranger at first, soon becomes a close father-figure and confidant to the narrator. Yet, the real father's death brings on feelings of guilt and remorse in the siblings; he is forgiven and granted new respect as his now grown-up children consider their past with deeper insight and understanding.

The spiritual values of the older generation, as reflected in this book, exclude any present-time trendy themes of violence or sexual obsessions; indeed, vitality and tension in a story can be achieved even better by means of gentle sensitivity and a more human approach.

In English

*More than One Life,* Alex Zucker, Lyn Coffin and Zdenka Brodská, trans., Evanston, Ill., Northwestern University Press, 1999.

# EGON HOSTOVSKÝ

## *Všeobecné spiknutí*
("The Plot")
New York, 1961

EGON HOSTOVSKÝ (1908–1973) was born to a family of Jewish industrialists. He worked at first as a publishers' editor and later as a Foreign Office official. In 1939, when the Nazis occupied his country, he was in Brussels, so he then proceeded to Paris, Lisbon and in 1941 to the United States. He returned to Prague after the war, only to return to exile after the communist *coup d'état*. From 1950 he lived in the US, first as a teacher of Czech language at the military school at Monterey, then as an advisor and editor at Radio Free Europe, and, eventually, as a freelance writer.

Already in the first Czechoslovak Republic he published two major prose works, *Případ profesora Körnera* ("Professor Körner's Case", 1932) and *Dům bez pána* ("A House without a Master", 1937), in which his introspective, uncertain and vulnerable protagonists act in unusual situations. From 1950, the themes of emigrés in the US are most frequent in his works. As he lived and wrote in the United States, they often appear in English earlier than in Czech. In Chicago his contemplative *Listy z vyhnanství* ("Letters from Exile") came out in 1941; *Cizinec hledá byt* ("A Foreigner Seeks a Flat") in 1947. In *Půlnoční pacient* ("The Midnight Patient", New York, 1954, in Czech, New York, Universum, 1959) Hostovský created a world of bizarre characters involved in espionage; the novel *Dobročinný večírek* ("The Charity Ball", London 1957, in Czech, New York, 1958) deals with the lives of emigrés in the fifties.

Generally, the world of Hostovský's novels includes themes of fascism, the Second World War, grotesque, tragic situations in human lives, the two-tier emigration (1939–45; post 1948), homelessness and duplicity. His most important novel, *Všeobecné spiknutí* (New York, 1961; in Czech, 1969) presents a complicated, exciting story situated in a world of both reality and delusion.

## The Plot

It is amazing how much action a writer can pack into a short time-span of three weeks. Hostovský's novel has 341 pages (Sixty-Eight Publishers, Toronto, 1973), a good deal of them "solid", that is, where narration prevails over direct speech; and yet, there is thrill and tension as in a detective story. In fact, it is a detective novel of a kind, as the title suggests – but the author's main concern is psychology, the mental state of his protagonist (who is also the main narrator), as he strives to preserve his sanity and to establish his identity.

The story takes place in the United States of America and the hero, Jan Bareš, is an exile. Hostovský himself was uprooted from his Czech homeland when it was occupied by the Nazis and later by the communists, and spent most of his exile years in the US; that is why he understood so well the often very painful process of mental adjustment in such radically different environments and situations in which his characters find themselves.

"The Plot" opens with a party at Bareš's flat, celebrating his 46th birthday. He is a writer, normally reserved rather than communicative, but this time he discloses to his friends all about his young days, in the idyllic part of his homeland in the north-east Bohemian border country. Throughout most of the 1930s the Czech and German population still lived there in peace. The strongest impression on the memory of this immature, somewhat diffident individualist is his unusual relationship with his bilingual schoolmates, Jiří Beck and Herbert Sturm. He sees them as role models rather than friends: the former, a radical (then secret) communist, the other a gentle aristocrat. The Munich agreement and subsequent war caused their paths to split: Beck survives the war, but Bareš never learns to know that during the later, hard Stalinist era he was sentenced and executed for his "deviating" views – a piece of information which the reader locates later in the novel. Herbert and his family leaves "heim ins Reich" with the other Sudeten-Germans and later serves the Nazi régime as a diplomat. During the war, his arrival in the occupied Bohemia and Moravia and the necessity to meet Bareš means a traumatic situation for the latter – while for the novelist it is an occasion to create a highly dramatic scene where a character no longer needed is removed: Sturm suffers a fatal heart attack just as he opens his arms to give Bareš a friendly embrace. All this is a brilliant piece of writing which could easily make a powerful psychological novel on its own.

As Bareš is telling his story, he becomes increasingly emotionally involved; this leads to his firm belief that he *saw* Beck, with his lady partner, at his party; but nobody else has seen him and the lady proves to be the wife of one of the guests. Not even the reader knows yet that Beck is dead. No wonder that the delusion makes Bareš's listeners worry about his mental health; their efforts to make him seek medical help turns them in his mind into his enemies, conspirators who plot to bring him to a mental hospital. Bareš fights back, especially when they try to take over the right of his own legal capacity, but, at the same time, he struggles with himself, for he does not behave as completely sane. The situation becomes crucial when his own, neat handwriting changes into Beck's untidy scrawl. Intrigues, mysteries, puzzling events – all full of suspense and excitement, follow abundantly, only to fall eventually into place like a complicated mosaic: clues lead to explanations, loose ends are phased out as the erring, somewhat self-pitying individualist finds in the end the needed refuge in the arms of his loving, devoted girlfriend whom he thought, up to now, that he didn't love.

This, however, does not mean a sugary happy end: the hero, actually, could not seriously attach himself to anybody; by implication, this kind of stability is the best Bareš can hope for. The way he learnt to love his girlfriend remains only a mystery in the novel full of people whose lives are frail and unpredictable.

"The Plot" is the work of a mature, experienced and quite prolific novelist. The themes of the exiles characterize his work best;[1] autobiographical elements serve well their veracity, but it is Hostovský's

---

[1] Cf. also *Letters from Exile; A Foreigner Seeks a Flat; The Midnight Patient.*

art to construct complicated plots which are at their best in this novel. He has made a name for himself in the western literary world at the time when a political barrier obscured the culture of his native country.

In English

*Letters from Exile,* Ann Krtil, trans., London, Allen and Unwin, 1942.

*The Hideout,* Fern Long, trans., New York, Random House, 1945.

*Missing,* Ewald Osers, trans., New York, Viking Press, 1952.

*The Midnight Patient,* Philip H. Smith, Jr., trans., Appleton-Century-Crofts, 1954.

*The Charity Ball,* Philip H. Smith, Jr., trans., London, Heinemann, 1957; New York, Doubleday, 1958.

*The Plot,* New York, 1961.

# BOHUMIL HRABAL

*Obsluhoval jsem anglického krále*
("I Served the King of England")
London, Chatto and Windus, 1989

*Listopadový uragán*
("The November Hurricane")
Prague, Tvorba-Delta, 1990

*The Death of Mr. Baltisberger*
London, Abacus, 1990

BOHUMIL HRABAL (1914–1997) was born in Brno where he attended grammar school, but completed this study at Český Brod. He read law in Prague (1935–39), interrupted by the war, and graduated 1946, simultaneously in literature, art and philosophy. As far as employment is concerned, he had a truly chequered career, as a clerk, railway signalman, insurance agent, general travelling agent, waste paper packer, theatre set shifter. He never practised as a lawyer, but became a professional writer in 1963. Like many Czech writers, he first wrote for literary journals; politically, some of his works could be published officially, while others came out only in *samizdat* or abroad. He wrote mostly prose which became very popular both at home and abroad, and many pieces were turned into plays and films.

His early short stories sound lyrical but already here he devel-

oped his typical style characterized by lively long sentences, colloquial, racy, even coarse language of his protagonists, the common
people who try to muddle through as best as they can, enjoying
good tales over mugs of beer in their pubs or homes. Hrabal is a born
raconteur who can hold his readers spellbound, as if they were
listening rather than reading.

Using his own life experiences as the main source of inspiration,
Hrabal grew into a prolific writer, so that only the most important
works can be listed here. First he wrote short stories, *Skřivánek na
niti* ("A Lark on a String", written 1959, but it was not allowed to
be published), and *Perlička na dně* ("A Pearl on the Bottom",
Prague, 1963). But it was the longer prose *Ostře sledované vlaky*
(Prague, Československý spisovatel, 1965; "Closely Observed
Trains") which has brought Hrabal his great popularity. In the same
year, short stories set in a Kafkaesque atmosphere of the fifties,
*Inserát na dům, ve kterém už nechci bydlet* ("Advertising the House
in Which I no Longer Wish to Live", 1965) came out.

It was only later that Hrabal – always witty, amusing and
immersed in his own past life – attempted to enrich his works with
philosophical argument (even in humorous contexts) and wrote a
few books of journalistic essays. Undoubtedly, the novel
*Obsluhoval jsem anglického krále* (written 1971, published in Köln,
Index, 1980; "I served the King of England" ) is his best, but perhaps
the trilogy in which Hrabal's art of autobiography culminates can
be described as his most monumental: *Svatby v domě* (Toronto,
Sixty-Eight Publishers, 1987), *Vita nuova* (Toronto, Sixty-Eight
Publishers, 1987), *Proluky* ("Remains"; Köln, Index, Purley,
Rozmluvy, Toronto, Sixty-Eight Publishers, 1986). In 1973 Hrabal
wrote but could not publish *Městečko, kde se zastavil čas* ("The
Little Town where Time Stood Still", 1993), a memoir of a life in
Nymburk where he spent his childhood. In fact, it is made up of tales
in which Hrabal's narrative style excels. *Příliš hlučná samota* ("Too
Loud a Solitude", Köln, Index, 1980) consists of a monologue of a
waste paper packer about precious books to be disposed of – the
ruthless way in which the communist régime was destroying the
cultural heritage of the nation.

Hrabal's essays, too, read well. They include *Listopadový uragán*
("The November Hurricane", Prague, Tvorba-Delta, 1990) and

*Něžní barbaři* ("Gentle Giants", Köln, Index, 1981), written mainly in honour of Hrabal's friend, the painter Vladimír Boudník.

## I Served the King of England

Hrabal's wartime novella *Ostře sledované vlaky* ("Closely Observed Trains", 1965) made his name known in the English-speaking world, especially when the film version appeared in 1973. He has written several works since, but his first full-length novel, *I Served the King of England,* shows his true expressive power. In his usual excessive mix of the naïve, the obscene, the absurd and the grotesque (perhaps too excessive for some readers, until they grasp the important functions of such elements), he allows his protagonist, the short and unattractive waiter Dítě, to narrate a fictionalized autobiography. In it the recurrent motif "I served the King of England" (and its variant "I served the Emperor of Abyssinia") helps to overcome his inferiority complex, although such glorious service came his way only once.

Dítě's touching story, a picaresque tale projected against a background of the turbulent events in Central Europe from the thirties to the fifties, recounts the useless struggle of an individual tossed about by circumstances. Illegitimate, abandoned by his mother and brought up by a nearly destitute grandmother who soon dies, Dítě must fend for himself. Full of *joie de vivre,* he sets out to be a millionaire and actually succeeds in doing so when he marries a Nazi fanatic who has appropriated a precious stamp collection from a transported Jew. When his wife gives birth to a cretinous child rather than the pure-blood Aryan they expected, the naïve Dítě suddenly discovers that he is considered by the Germans as inferior and by the Czechs as an upstart, and interloper among the rich, who never accept him. The communists deprive him of everything, then send him to jail and afterwards to hard labour in the forests. He ends up as a solitary road mender in a deserted hut in the devastated Sudetenland, a stark solitude in which he can come to terms with himself, forgotten by all. His few domestic animals are now more precious to him than his millions.

Like his predecessor Jaroslav Hašek, Hrabal is an excellent raconteur. His endless stream-of-consciousness sentences running

on for pages at a stretch without paragraph breaks or direct speech
look formidable, but are actually quite clear and readable. There is,
in fact, a constant sense of listening rather than reading. Hrabal's
robust humour has contributed to his fame, and here it is very much
in evidence, as in the scene where Dítě's breeding capacity is being
tested by the racist Germans before he is allowed to marry Lise. The
many interpolated stories, tall tales and passages of pure horseplay
cannot conceal the underlying seriousness of intent. Gargantuan
feasts and rampant promiscuity are obscured by the gloomy faces of
German soldiers leaving for the front, and there are also the transport trains filled with Jews going in one direction and with prisoners
and the wounded going in the other; add the destruction of Lidice,
the horrors of a blitz, and the inhumanity of the communist régime,
and the result is a world wherein a little human grub who knows no
better is simply trodden upon and ground to nothing.

## Listopadový uragán

Hurricanes are rare in Central Europe, but political events do
sweep the region like those merciless storms. Having in mind the
"December hurricane", an 1897 Jewish pogrom in Prague, Hrabal
uses the title "November Hurricane" for this publication, written
during and referring to the events of 1989 in his native Czechoslovakia. It was on 17th November of that year when a "hurricane"
in the form – paradoxically enough – of the "Velvet Revolution"
caused the communist régime to crumble, but the change of the
political climate had already been felt earlier. Hrabal's collection of
ten pieces records the atmosphere subtly.

The opening part, "The Magic Flute", sets the tone with a kind
of memoir in which the author tries to find his soul, his place as
both a writer and a human being, in the changing society. In his
self-examination he sounds apologetic in justifying his refusal to
join the dissidents in spite of his sympathy with them, particularly
with their leader Václav Havel. In the following piece Hrabal
seems to be experimenting with the epistolary form: an imaginary
female narrator-recorder addresses the author himself, but eight
letters are directed to Hrabal's American friend April Clifford. His
tender feelings for this young Californian Slavist serve as a thread

that leads him to a lecture tour of American universities, including Stanford where Clifford works, and sparks vivid descriptions of his strong impressions from this world, so new to him. He tells her all sorts of things, about himself and his work; about numerous Czechs in North America; about Havel, Dubček; about his drinking companions; and about literature and art. He adds a gentle touch by writing with great affection about his many cats. His narrative proves fascinating: it is amusing and witty, but also personal in its sincerely expressed doubts, guilt, and pain as the muddled world affects him.

Hrabal's American experience contrasts sharply with life and events at home. Beer flows in this publication as usual, although much less than in his earlier works, and it is now drunk with greater serenity. One can also recognize the author's typical style in the protracted, often grammatically incorrect sentences, which in no way impede his fluent narrative stream. In all, "November Hurricane" is an interesting and pleasant personal chronicle of 1989 by a gifted, experienced writer.

## *The Death of Mr. Baltisberger*

This collection of fourteen short stories shows Hrabal as a true pupil of Jaroslav Hašek in the art of the beerhouse tale, but a pupil who has also advanced and rejuvenated the genre through experimentation and innovation. Typically, beer flows freely in many of the stories and mugs swish along the countertop as the skilful barmaid slides them expertly into customers' hands. And of course, people tell tales, tall ones and often absurd, but that is precisely the idea: the spoiled reader must be shocked by the unexpected if his interest is to last. He will be amply rewarded if he reads on, for he will get many more than just fourteen stories, often finding several intertwined within a single selection as the characters compete in recounting their respective tales. In the title story the excited, yarn-spinning raconteurs who come from great distances to applaud Mr. Baltisberger in the running of the Brno Grand Prix miss the tragedy of his death altogether. In "Diamond Eye" the absurd and the comic combine in a policeman's gratitude towards his assailant: "You see, before Papa hit him, his nose had been bent over to the right. And

Papa's punch straightened it so nicely that the daughter of a rich farmer fell in love with him and they got married."

Hrabal's characters are very ordinary people, mostly just casual acquaintances. Baltisberger was apparently a real-life race driver killed in the Grand Prix, however, and Uncle Pepin in the same story was evidently modelled on the author's own uncle. Throughout this collection Hrabal appears as a great raconteur with an amazing imagination and a gift for creating unexpected images: "His eyes were rimmed with red, like a telegram form"; "The young man was as deeply immersed in himself as a collapsible sewing machine". Combined with his earthy humour and the grotesque or absurd situations in which he often places his characters, this quality makes the stories eminently readable.

In English

*Closely Observed Trains,* Edith Pargeter, trans., London, Jonathan Cape, 1968.

*I Served the King of England,* Paul Wilson, trans., London, Chatto and Windus, 1989.

*Too Loud a Solitude,* Michael Henry Heim, trans., San Diego, Harcourt Brace Yovanovich, 1990.

*The Death of Mr. Baltisberger,* Michael Henry Heim, trans., London, Abacus, 1990. Original Czech title: *Automa Svět.*

*Cutting it Short (Postřižiny), The Little Town where Time Stood Still,* James Naughton, trans., London, Abacus, 1993.

*Dancing Lessons for the Advanced in Age,* Michael Henry Heim, trans., London, Harvill, 1998.

*Letters to Dubenka,* James Naughton, trans., Prague, Twisted Spoon Press, 1998. Czech title: *Listopadový Uragán.*

# EVA KANTŮRKOVÁ

## *Nečas*
### Prague, Hynek, 2000

EVA KANTŮRKOVÁ, born 1930 in Prague, is a fiction writer, essayist and scriptwriter. She studied philosophy and history in Prague and worked later with the communist youth as their organizer and editor of their newspaper. Ideologically, this was due to the influence of her communist father, but, in the sixties when she started writing (her mother was a writer, too), and especially after the Soviet invasion in 1968, her political views changed. She joined the dissidents, signed the Charter 77 and published abroad a book of interviews with women persecuted for political reasons, *Sešly jsme se v této knize* ("We Have Met in this Book", 1980). The last event resulted in her being imprisoned without trial for ten months, 1981–82. After the Velvet Revolution in 1989 she entered public life as an MP, President of the Writers' Union and as a member of staff of the Ministry of Culture. Most of her early works were published in *samizdat* and abroad.

In her first, very successful, novel, *Smuteční slavnost* ("The Funeral", 1967), she is concerned with the death of a farmer, victim of the communist collectivization of agriculture in the fifties. His funeral rouses the conscience of those who had earlier selfishly exploited the situation when they confiscated his property, but it is too late – and nature itself avenges the victim. The novel was adapted for the screen, but could not be officially shown until 1990, after the fall of the régime.

After two books of short stories, *Pozůstalost pana Abela* ("Mr. Abel's Legacy", 1977) and *Člověk v závěsu* ("In the Limbo", 1988), followed a loosely connected trilogy, *Po potopě* ("After the Deluge", 1969), *Černá hvězda* ("The Black Star", 1982), depicting the painful disillusionment with politics of a pre-war communist journalist, a character inspired by her father) and *Zahrada dětství jménem Eden* ("The Childhood Garden called Eden", 1998). The theme of disappointment in politics – some kind of confrontation between communism and Christianity – appears already in the novels *Pán věže* ("The Master of the Tower", 1992) and in the historical sketch *Jan Hus* (1988) where the great reformer represents the exemplary "life in truth".

In *Přítelkyně z domu smutku* ("My Companions in Bleak House", 1984) the author records her experiences from the prison; the publication was translated into several languages, appeared on the television and was awarded the Tom Stoppard prize.

Recently Kantůrková has published two books of memoirs, *Památník* ("An Album", 1994) and *Záznamy paměti* ("Notes in Memory", 1997), which were followed by two volumes of diaries, *Nejsi* ("You are no More", 1999) and *Nečas* (2000).

## *Nečas*

Kantůrková's latest works spring from her grief at her husband's death. She tried to find solace in writing her diary, published as *Nejsi* ("You are no More"), to grasp how his absence affected her efforts to come to terms with the sad fact; in *Nečas,* he is still very much a part of her, a silent companion to whom she can turn with a question, comment or recollection. She proposes to compile a book about a fictitious novelist called Nečas, who constructs his own novel, that is, she is writing "a novel about a novel".

It seems that the late husband may participate in the novel somehow, perhaps the fictitious Nečas has some of his characteristics. His continual presence in the author's mind determines the emotional atmosphere and leads to the unusual, complicated form of the novel. The character of Nečas gradually emerges through his own compilation of the plot. He considers numerous suggestions which are either accepted or rejected, by the author, or through her by the late husband – in fact, the pages of the book are teeming with question marks. The events do not follow in a direct line, yet the drama emerges in Nečas' mind as a search for the identity of his wife Věra who was drowned in the sea on her way from Holland to England.

This tragic end of his happy marriage raises many questions, doubts and suspicions for Nečas. Věra, very interested in the culture of the Celts, was awarded a grant to go and study the subject abroad, and paid a visit to her friend in Amsterdam on her way to England (presumably to Wales and Ireland): did she do so to meet also her possible lover ("the tormentor" who causes suffering to both Věra and Nečas)? And how did she die? For his novel Nečas rejects the idea of a small boat hired by Věra and her friend, wrecked by a stormy sea, but a sinking ferry (like the real one in Zeebrugge not so long ago) is more plausible for his purpose. Věra's body is never found, only her handbag containing her notebook is later discovered on a faraway English shore. In his search for Věra's soul Nečas examines the notebook, even plunges into the study of the Celts. She appears in his dreams and, in view of the Celtic mythology, he wonders if he could contact her through a spiritualist medium. As he is imagining her in various situations, he creates in his mind an image of her, more exact than he actually saw her before.

In contacting people who knew Věra, precious information is gained, particularly through the subtle relationship of Nečas with the teen-age Olga, Věra's daughter from her first marriage, whom he hardly knew before. He takes the girl to Amsterdam and allows her to tear the notebook sheet by sheet and throw it to the sea from a steamer; but, no, that's not good enough: the relic must be burnt by him on a little bonfire as he used to make with Věra in the same place near their Czech country holiday home. This happens when Nečas appears more reconciled with the loss of his beloved wife, who seems "to have flown through his life like a burning star, extinguished by the sea" (p. 160).

Through the method of creating a character who constructs his novel Kantůrková introduces the reader to her own workshop. As she "discusses" the variations of Nečas' potential novel's plot with her late husband (and through him with the reader), it develops slowly as it gets entangled, but clarity emerges in the end from her own loneliness. She grants the hero the final peace and reconciliation almost grudgingly when she concludes Nečas with: "But whom can I tell that I am frightened?"

The book is a fine piece of writing, dealing most subtly with human emotions and relations.

In English

*My Companions in the Bleak House,* anonymous trans., London, Quartet, 1989.

# IVAN KLÍMA

## *Waiting for the Dark, Waiting for the Light*
Translated by Paul Wilson, Granta/Penguin, 1994

## *Ani svatí ani andělé*
("No Saints or Angels")
Prague, Hynek, 1999

IVAN KLÍMA was born in 1931. His childhood was scarred by his enforced stay for over three years in the ghetto at Terezín (1941–1945). This experience set up a tone of gloom, fear and uncertainty in his writings. He studied Czech and the theory of literature at Prague University and worked afterwards as editor of books and leading journals. He displeased the communist régime by joining the dissidents; although he was allowed to go to the United States for six months (1969–70) as a visiting lecturer at the University of Michigan, he lost his post in Prague after his return. His books were banned and he had to earn his living by menial work. Frustrating as this may have been, it inspired Klíma to write short stories in which such themes could be treated with humour and irony. Needless to say, between 1970 and 1989 he could publish only in *samizdat* or abroad.

He was strongly influenced by Karel Čapek whom he was the first to raise from the neglect caused by both the Nazis and the communists. His dissertation on Čapek came out in 1962 (still "officially" in the state publishing house, Československý spisovatel) to be re-written more than once and appearing in its final form in 2001 in Prague as *Velký věk chce mít též velké mordy* and in English in the US in 2002 as *Karel Čapek, Life and Work* (Catbird Press, North Haven, CT).

Klíma is known as a successful playwright and essayist, but his fiction, especially the short stories, prevails in number: *Bezvadný den* ("A Wonderful Day", 1960), *Milenci na jednu noc* ("Lovers for one Night", 1964), *Loď jménem Naděje* ("A Ship Called 'Hope'", 1969), *Milenci na jeden den* ("Lovers for one Day", 1970), *Má veselá jitra* ("My Merry Mornings", Toronto, 1971), *Moje první lásky* ("My First Loves", Toronto, 1985), *Moje zlatá řemesla* ("My Golden Trades", Prague 1990) and *Moje nebezpečné výlety* ("My Dangerous Trips", 2004). Characters who try to improve their lives in the dreary atmosphere of political oppression appear in these stories, but in his novels human relationships are dealt with in more depth.

The first, *Hodina ticha* ("A Peaceful Hour"), already published in 1963, can be described as a socio-philosophical novel, with the plot situated in Slovakia; *Milostné léto* ("A Summer Affair", Toronto, 1979) is concerned with human frailty, loneliness and love. *Soudce z milosti* ("Judge on Trial", London, 1986) is about the problems of a judge, who, checked by the régime, cannot carry out sentences freely according to his conscience. The hero of *Láska a smetí* ("Love and Garbage", London, 1988) is a writer working as a road sweeper, who tries to come to terms with his past life and his present relationship with people – his wife and his lover, a sculptress. *Čekání na tmu, čekání na světlo* ("Waiting for the Dark, Waiting for the Light", 1993) depicts a young man's disappointment with the situation shortly after the Velvet Revolution 1989. *Poslední stupeň důvěrnosti* ("Ultimate Intimacy", 1996) tries to solve – not very convincingly – the two main problems of a Protestant clergyman, his almost obsessive love to a rather uncongenial mistress, and his loss of faith. *Ani svatí ani andělé* ("No Saints or Angels", 1999) draws successfully a truthful picture of the evils by which Czech society is trapped in the early days of building a better future in the new political freedom.

Klíma's writings often show autobiographical aspects: the trauma of the ghetto and fear of death linger in it. He uses interior monologue to advantage; the contemporary society to which he belonged from the wartime through the communist dictatorship and its legacy after 1989 gave inspiration to his creative, contemplative mind. He is one of the most outstanding Czech contemporary writers.

## Waiting for the Dark, Waiting for the Light

This book, with its layered structure and interweaving of the single episodes, is reminiscent of James Joyce; yet, the combination of dream and reality has a distinctive, gloomy, Kafkaesque tang. The "dark" period for the TV cameraman Pavel is that dominated by the long-lived communist régime; it is a time during which he can only dream about his own great, uncensored screenplay. Through his own fault he loses the woman he loves; he then sleeps with another because he cannot live with his senile mother, whom he visits and cares for loyally. His experiences, rather ordinary, but including a jail term after an unsuccessful attempt to flee the country, are projected in his fictitious screenplay into a drama full of thrill, tension and tragedy.

Under the old régime, Pavel keeps his comparatively good job in a minimal show of conformity. Has he betrayed his ideals? he wonders. Following the Velvet Revolution, the question arises as to whether he is now one of " the poisoners". He is not dismissed, but feels utterly alienated among the new people around him. He leaves voluntarily and, with friends, starts a private advertising company. The world of consumerism only increases his alienation, as he finds the price of independence to be rather high: the early pressure to sing the communist tune has only changed into the pressure to eulogize "ever-sharp kitchen knives, ketchup and chewing gum". The darkness has not turned to light for Pavel, and his gloom grows into pessimism , even nihilism, in his now almost surrealist dream screenplay. Clearly, he "lacked hope".

Psychologically, Klíma has drawn an admirably deep portrait of an ordinary citizen under communism and his hapless emergence from under its sway. The novel's unusual structure gives it its artistic frame. The author's style and language are powerful, abounding in symbolic images, not always of lame jays (in the semtex factory) or ravens looking "like black crosses floating in the sky", which truly bring darkness into the book. But is Pavel a true representative of the nation's mood? one wonders. There may be quite a few who have not fully realized that there is a price to pay for freedom, and the wounds inflicted upon human souls by the previous régime's poison cannot be healed overnight. But, surely, life is not quite so hopeless?

## Ani svatí, ani andělé

The effects of Klíma's traumatic childhood experiences under the Nazis appear in this book, intensified into a serious concern and search for the causes of unhappiness in human relations. A decade after the fall of communism in Klíma's homeland the destructive legacy of the odious régime still upsets indirectly the balance of normality in this excellent analysis of the fact that not everything is well in the renewed democracy as yet.

The heroine, Kristýna, still feels the shadow of her father's communist past, as well as his misbehaviour towards her mother; she, herself, no saint, but not great sinner either, is just an ordinary, fallible, vulnerable being, a dentist by profession and inclined to suffer from depression. Although attractive and longing for a stable relationship, she seems unable to attain one: her husband leaves her and their young daughter, to whom she then gives all her attention. Later, however, unaware of the danger, she fails to prevent the adolescent girl from falling in with bad company and becoming a drug addict of the lowest kind. Finding solace in the genuine love and support of a man much younger than herself, Kristýna ultimately cannot keep him. Her anxiety about curing her daughter's addiction provides the core and tension in the book, with the redeeming aspect of the daughter's ultimate return to normal life.

A number of successfully drawn minor characters complete the scene. Although some of them are not old enough to remember the darkest periods of the old régime, they still seem to be subconsciously guarding their sense of self-preservation at any price. Kristýna's young admirer, who works in a government office and has access to reports of agents working for the communists, gets closest to the evil. His attempts to remedy the wrongs prove futile for lack of evidence or inadequacy of the law. But he was no Messiah, neither saint nor angel, and he disappears quietly from Kristýna's life.

The novel is an excellent piece of writing, as the author uses interior monologue almost exclusively. This allows the reader to look closely into the characters' deepest thoughts and feelings; however horrifying, the teenager's remarkable realistic idiom gives the novel a streak of comedy. The sequence of the chapters, alternating between the three main characters – Kristýna, her young admirer and her daughter – provides the ebb and flow, like the pulsating rhythm in human life. In this novel Klíma has created a powerful picture of postcommunist Czech society at the close of the millennium.

In English

*My Merry Mornings,* George Theiner, trans., London, New York, Readers International, 1985.

*My First Loves,* Ewald Osers, trans., London, Penguin, 1986, 1989.

*A Summer Affair,* Ewald Osers, trans., London, Penguin, 1987.

*Love and Garbage,* Ewald Osers, trans., London, Penguin, 1990.

*My Golden Trades,* Paul Wilson, trans., London, Granta, 1992.

*The Spirit of Prague,* Paul Wilson, trans., London, Granta/Penguin, 1994.

*Waiting for the Dark, Waiting for the Light,* Paul Wilson, trans., London, Granta/Penguin, 1994.

*The Ultimate Intimacy,* A. G. Brain, trans., London, Granta, 1997.

*Lovers for a Day,* Gerald Turner, trans., London, Granta, 1999.

*Between Security and Insecurity,* Gerald Turner, trans., London, Thames and Hudson, 2000.

*Karel Čapek,* Norma Comrada, trans., North Haven CT, Catbird Press, 2001.

*Judge on Trial,* A. G. Brain, trans., London, Vintage, 2002.

# PAVEL KOHOUT

## *Kde je zakopán pes*
### ("Where the Dog is Buried")
#### Cologne, Index, 1987

PAVEL KOHOUT (born 1928) studied comparative literature at the Faculty of Philosophy at Charles University in Prague, but changed his subject in the second year to aesthetics and drama. He held important cultural posts, in the broadcasting corporation, television, as a journals' editor, even in diplomatic service as a cultural attaché in Moscow (1949–1950). As a leader and representative of youth organizations he was able to travel abroad comparatively frequently until he was expelled from the communist party in 1969. Then his works were blacklisted, too, so that he could publish only in *samizdat* or abroad. By now, however, he had made a name for himself abroad as a dramatist, especially in Germany and Austria, where his plays were translated, published and performed in German. Legally, the régime could not charge him, but he was harassed, interrogated and, in 1979, not allowed to return home from his officially permitted visit to Vienna.

Kohout wrote poetry and prose, but his plays and dramatizations of other writers' works prevail in number. His prose writings, which mostly satirize the absurdities and atrocities of the "normalization", originate in the post-1968 period. Inventing grotesque, farcical situations and using eccentric, baffling metaphors, Kohout created in his works a world of the true tragicomedy to which the lives of ordinary people (the dissidents in the first place) were reduced.

Most of these prose works came out first in German: *Z deníku kontrarevolucionáře* ("The Diary of a Counter-revolutionary",

Luzern, 1969), *Bílá kniha o kauze Adam Juráček* ("The White Book on the Case on Adam Juráček", Luzern, 1970; in Czech: Toronto, Sixty-Eight Publishers, 1978), *Katyně* ("The Hangwoman", Luzern, 1978, in Czech: Cologne, Index, 1980), *Nápady svaté Kláry* ("Saint Clara's Ideas", Luzern, 1980, in Czech: Toronto, Sixty-Eight Publishers, 1982), *Kde je zakopán pes* ("Where the Dog is Buried", Munich, 1987, in Czech: Cologne, Index, 1987), *Hodina tance a lásky* ("An Hour of Dance and Love", Munich, 1989, in Czech: Cologne, Index, 1989). Only *Hvězdná hodina vrahů* ("A Starry Hour of Murderers") and *Konec velkých prázdnin* ("The End of a Great Vacation") could be published in Prague, free again, in 1995 and 1996 respectively.

## *Kde je zakopán pes*

This work has the subtitle "a memoir-novel"; in spite of the fictional implication, it is a very important and most detailed document about the troubled lives of the Czech dissidents during the totalitarian régime. The author may not have been the most persecuted of them, but where he didn't share, he saw the harassment which those involved had to suffer, harassment which really existed but may seem incredible to the younger generation, brought up in democracy.

A novel as a fictional form usually has a protagonist and other characters, while a memoir is expected to be truthful; to reconcile both, there is Pavel Kohout himself, his wife and family as well as a host of their dissident friends, all under their real names, acting as they did in their real lives. The author, as the main narrator, brightens his diary entries by turning to their pet dog as the main listener. Actually, this little dachshund, much loved by his owners and most by Kohout's wife, gave the book its title "Where the Dog is Buried", for, after having played his part, he is really eventually buried, being brutally poisoned by the spiteful police. The symbolic meaning of the fact can hardly be overlooked: other innocent animals in the garden and adjoining fields perish through the spreading poison – like many human victims of the corrupt régime.

The book consists of diary entries on two time levels: one, registering in detail events between 11 July 1978 and 28 October 1978, the other looking back to the years 1961–70, to the circumstances which eventually led to the most serious persecution of the signatories of the Charter 77, as they are described in the first time level.

The year 1978 was very distressful for Kohout, when a particular incident gave his memoir-novel its plot: as in a novel, the memoir flows right through the work, giving it at times the character of a detective story, and getting disentangled at the end by a sad, but probably life-saving, enforced stay in the exile for Kohout and his wife. After several instances of harassment, dating approximately from 1971, in the summer 1978 Kohout was intimidated by a threatening letter, asking him to deliver an exorbitant amount of money to a secret place. What else could he do for his security but turn to the criminal police for protection? This powerful body pretended to take action, but it only proved useless, for the letter was their own trick to get Kohout – with impunity – under their surveillance. A strong street lamp was installed at the gate of his house outside Prague, patrol cars of his "guard" circled round, then he was directly accused of having criticized Stalin. An undetected arsonist caused fire in his house – but the worst followed after Kohout signed the Charter 77: in the vicinity of the Prague castle his wife was attacked and abducted, while Kohout himself received – obviously through the police – 128 threatening letters in two days; his new car was deliberately immobilized; the brakes of his wife's little Fiat unexpectedly failed and a bomb was later found in it. Kohout's flat in Prague was confiscated and their pet dog had to pay with his life, when the régime couldn't genuinely accuse his master of any illegal activity.

The Chartists 77 gained a lot of effective sympathy from the cultural and political circles in the western countries so that Czech blacklisted authors could publish their works abroad if they could not do so in their homeland. Kohout has earned himself a good reputation as a dramatist, particularly in West Germany and Austria, and he also enjoyed the friendship of the Swiss Ambassador – all this helped to check the persecution to a certain extent, but did not diminish the acrimony of the persecutors. Tension in the book persists; the author's ironic or bitter tone being sweetened by the mutual loyalty and solidarity of the dissidents, by the love and affection among the family members and, last but not least, by their tender feelings for their pet dog (a budgerigar, too), the symbol of human cruelty as well as the absurdity of the totalitarian system.

Whether a novel or a document, the book is a testimony of one tragic period in the history of the Czech nation, when brave individuals defended the spiritual ideals of democracy against their most powerful infamous enemy.

In English

*I am Snowing.* The Confessions of a Woman of Prague, Czech original title: *Sněžím,* Neil Bermel, trans., New York, Farrar, Strauss and Giroux, 1994.

# FRANTISEK KOŽÍK

## *Po zarostlém chodníčku*
("On an Overgrown Path")
Prague, Československý spisovatel, 1967

FRANTISEK KOŽÍK (1909–1997) was the son of a judge and an actress. He studied law (JUDr. 1931) and, simultaneously, also dramatic arts at the conservatoire. Very soon he started writing for leading periodicals and gradually wrote an amazing number of scenarios and plays for radio. He published a few volumes of lyric poetry celebrating nature, as well as many books for children and the young. Towards the end of the thirties his interest took the direction towards history, especially the notable personalities, the history-makers. Inspired by the fashionable *biographie romancée* which flourished then in Europe, he enriched Czech literature as he became the most popular representative of this genre. Although the famous critic F. X. Šalda disliked this literary form for being neither art nor fact, Kožík's knowledge was well equipped with facts so that his readers were not misled – and he could join fact and fiction very successfully. In fact, the proportion of these two elements varies from one book to another, including some almost purely historical works, like *Kronika života a vlády Karla IV, krále českého a císaře římského* ("The Chronicle of the Life and Reign of Charles IV, King of Bohemia and Emperor of the Holy Roman Empire", 1981) or *Blázny živí bůh* (1969, rewritten 1969, "God Looks after the Fools"), about travelling actors in mediaeval Flanders.

Although the subjects of Kožík's biographical novels come from various walks of life, artists attracted him most. His first, *Největší z Pierotů* ("The Greatest among Pierrots", 1939), about the French

mime of Czech origin, Caspar Deburau, who achieved his glory by
his art, established Kožík as a very successful writer. Then followed
*Básník neumírá* ("The Poet never Dies", 1940) about the Portuguese
16th century poet Luis de Camões; *Josef Mánes* (1955) about the
classic Czech painter of 19th century; *Bolestný a hrdinský život Jana
Amose Komenského* ("The Sorrowful and Heroic Life of Jan Amos
Komenský", 1958) about the 17th century Czech theologian,
philosopher and educationalist, rewritten in 1970 as *Světlo v
temnotách*, "Light in Darkness" and translated into English and
French as "Johan Amos Comenius"; *Pouta věrnosti* ("The Bounds
of Loyalty", 1971) about the painter Jaroslav Čermák, end of 19th
and beginning of 20th century; *Miláček národa* ("The Nation's
Darling", 1975) about the 19th century dramatist and actor Josef
Kajetán Tyl.

In the following works fact prevails over fiction: *Na křídle
větrného mlýna* ("On the Wing of a Windmill",1977) and *Neklidné
babí léto* ("The Unquiet Indian Summer", 1979), both dealing with
the life of the painter Zdenka Braunerová; also in *Fanfáry pro krále*
("Fanfares for the King", 1983) to honour the great actor Eduard
Vojan, and *Věnec vavřínový* ("A Laurel Wreath") celebrating the
life of Dr. Miroslav Tyrš, founder of Sokol, the physical education
institution based on the *callocagathia* principle, 1962.

Sometimes Kožík modified the way of his writing: for example,
he used a few narrators in the pen portrait of Miguel de Cervantes
Saavedra, *Rytíř smutné postavy* ("The Mournful Knight Errant",
1958) and in *Po zarostlém chodníčku* (1967) he included personal
memories and testimonies referring to the life of Leoš Janáček. And
Kožík did not forget the sportsmen: the hero of *Vítěz maratonský*
("The Marathon Winner", 1952) is the runner Emil Zátopek.

## *Po zarostlém chodníčku*

Among the varieties of Kožík's biographies, "On an Overgrown
Path", entitled after one of Janáček's most intimate compositions, is
not really a novel, but a study with details based on facts and in many
cases on authentic quotations; the writer has added "only as much
psychology as one can find in Janáček's own words". Yet, his skill
as a lucid writer of fiction adds much charm to this work.

The author plunges immediately into the middle of the composer's life, describing the illness and death of his dearly loved daughter Olga. The tone of sadness and bitterness is increased by Janáček's vain efforts to win recognition among composers; his style was misunderstood, and Prague kept refusing to perform his works. It is only the following chapters that go back to his earlier life, and Kožík continues with evocations of the more cheerful events which led eventually to Janáček's success.

Kožík collected his material from written records and from the memories of Janáček's contemporaries who knew him; consequently, descriptive chapters alternate with rather journalistic interviews, a method which adds both authenticity and liveliness to the book. The picture of Janáček's personality is quite clear – and a lay music enthusiast will not be bored by the excess of technicalities. Kožík's admiration of the great composer is not blurred by partiality; along with the references to the composer's kindness, patience and efficiency no secret is made of his hot temper and occasional unjust actions, nor of women other than his wife having inspired Janáček to his greatest works. In this respect we owe most to the twenty-six-year-old Mrs. Kamila Stössl, with whom Janáček fell in love when he was in his sixties. Quotations from his letters to her leave no doubt about the depth of his feelings, but her own and her husband's attitudes remain rather obscure, in spite of the long duration of their good relationship. Is it because Kožík felt, perhaps, that this part belonged rather to a biographical novel – with which this study of Janáček has not much in common?

In English

*The Sorrowful and Heroic Life of John Amos Comenius,* Prague, Státní pedagogické nakladatelství (State Educational Publishing House), 1958.

# IVAN KRAUS

## *Rodinný sjezd*
### ("Family Reunion")
Prague, Marsyas, 1996

IVAN KRAUS' (born 1939) parents were clerks, but the family was also involved in the arts: writing (father, Ivan); acting (mother, brother, Ivan); puppet-acting (Ivan's sister-in-law). Although Ivan studied commerce, he became at first an actor and scriptwriter in a good number of minor variety theatres. He left the communist Czechoslovakia in 1968, moving often from one country to another: Switzerland, Italy, France, Bahamas, Britain, Germany and France again. In exile he worked as a scriptwriter for the radio and television (BBC, Radio Free Europe, German and French national broadcasting corporations), as well as an independent writer. He has found the short story to be his main genre. Single items of this kind came out in numerous periodicals at first, but later also in book form: *To na tobě doschne* ("This will Get Dry on You", Zurich, 1976), *Prosím tě, neblázni* ("Please, don't get Mad", Zurich, 1978), *Číslo do nebe* ("The Number for Heaven", Zurich, 1984), *Výhodné nabídky aneb Život na Západě* ("Special Offers, or the Life in the West", Prague, 1992), *Nejchytřejší národ na světě* ("The Cleverest Nation in the World", Prague, 1994). In 2001 he published *Kůň nežere okurkový salát* ("A Horse Does not Eat Cucumber Salad"), a novelette about a Ph.D. graduate returning from abroad to his native country. In fact, after the Velvet Revolution a number of his publications came out: *Číslo do nebe* ("A Number for Heaven", 2000), *Muž za vlastním rohem* ("A Man Round his Own Corner, 2000), *Snídaně v poledne* ("A Brunch", 2002), *Muž pod vlastním dohledem* ("The Man Supervised by Himself, 2002), *Medová léta* ("Honey-sweet Years", 2003), *Udělej mi tichoučko* ("Make Silence for me", 2003).

Kraus' stories are very amusing, full of comic, bizarre scenes acted by peculiar, grotesque characters – as if Kraus could poke fun almost at anybody, including himself. In a number of his stories the absurdities of the totalitarian régimes have become the target of his witty irony and sarcasm. As he favours the theme of family relations, he takes his part in the stories, thus making them lively, as if he was taking the reader into his confidence.

## *Rodinný sjezd*

In his book on the short story T. O. Beachcroft saw the genre as "modest art", which well befits Ivan Kraus' truly modest (as far as size is concerned) "Family Reunion", a slim book of nineteen short stories. It is good to see this modest but challenging art being favoured by "a specialist" who has already published several volumes of witty short stories, showing clearly how much one can make out of comparatively small means: in this collection Kraus' own family provided all the material he needed to express, with humour, but in no uncertain terms, what was happening to ordinary human beings during the Nazi occupation and under communist rule.

The family reunion takes place in better times, when the worst is over, but the past experiences of each member of this Jewish family still linger in their subconscious and affect their actions: a gift of luxury shoes for the father recalls the scene in the concentration camp where prisoners, the "Schuhläufer", had to walk aimlessly in good new shoes in order to make them comfortable for the soldiers; an indifference with which a guest in a café drinks "polinaris mineral water" brings to the father's mind the life-giving effect of this same brand of water when he lay very sick in the same camp; forty years later he could buy a bottle himself and present it with gratitude to the friendly inmate who saved his life back then.

Gruesome as the stories of the past may be, Kraus does not moan; on the contrary, in retrospect he sees the comic side of the situations which he describes with subtle irony, so that the horrid past is revealed through witty observations: the child who lives in a world of fairy tales sees the SS men as warlocks who had thrown his father into a dungeon while the evil witch was lighting the fire in the furnace; when communism disperses the family to various corners of the western world, the father, although glad about the children's safety, resents his favourite daughter's incompetent way of defecting by marrying a Colombian (rather than an American) – an excellent man, as the father later finds out; the thought of Kafka's works, readily available abroad but on the blacklist in the writer's communist homeland, leads to a comparison of communist management to Kafka's turbulent world.

Slim as the book may be, the stories fall gracefully into place to give a clear, vivid portrait of a truly cosmopolitan family, gathering after many years of forced separation; they speak Czech, English, Spanish and German, always with someone interpreting, so that the new family relatives from across the wide world might understand. *Rodinný sjezd* is an enjoyable book, using gentle humour to convey serious thoughts about life.

# JAN KŘESADLO

## *Mrchopěvci*
### ("Funeral Singers")
Toronto, Sixty-Eight Publishers, 1984, 1990

JAN KŘESADLO (1926–1995) is the pen-name of Václav Pinkava, Csc.,Ph.D., an exceptionally gifted polymath. He was not only a writer, but also a word-play-loving linguist, composer (church music, folk song arrangements), painter and scholarly scientist. His inborn outspokenness brought about difficulties in his education: in 1944 the Nazis did not allow him to finish his grammar school years (the "Classical Gymnasium" where he gained his good knowledge of Greek and Latin); he could do so only after the war. As soon as the communists seized power, he had to leave his university course in Philosophy and English. After his National Service he was accepted to study Psychology at the Charles University in Prague, 1951–54. From 1961 he worked at the Prague University Teaching Hospital Outpatient Clinic for sexual deviations; he left the country in 1968 and settled in Colchester as a clinical psychologist.

In his writings Křesadlo developed a unique style, interspersed here and there by passages in foreign languages, including minority languages and dialects (apart from Latin and Greek: German, Hungarian, Slovak, Roma, border country German dialect . . . ). His prose – thrilling, provocative, bizarre, even irreverent – abounds in black humour, horror, absurdities and morbidity; his dealing with clinical cases of sexual deviations has necessarily stimulated his vivid imagination. Although he started writing comparatively late in life, his literary achievement is truly respectable. While his work among mentally disturbed people became the main source of his inspiration

(*Mrchopěvci,* "Funeral Singers", Toronto, Sixty-Eight Publishers, 1984; short stories collection *Slepá bohyně,* "The Blind Goddess", Prague, Art Service, 1991), he also saw ideologies like Nazism and communism as outcomes of twisted minds of their adherents; in fact, he could debunk any behaviour which seemed to him unreasonable, pompous or ill-judged. In *Fuga trium* (Toronto, Sixty-Eight Publishers, 1988) he created a world of a triple escape from the absurd political reality; his *Obětina* ("A Sacrifice", Prague, Ivo Železný, 1994) is an iconoclastic and linguistic extravaganza in a complicated triple structure including a parody of a gothic romance, written partly in verse. In *Vara guru* (Toronto, Sixty-Eight Publishers, 1989) he is concerned not so much with politics, but rather with the bizarre characters at a Czech aristocrat's estate during the economic depression of the thirties.

*Zámecký pán aneb antikuro* ("The Lord of the Manor", Prague, Ivo Železný, 1992) was inspired by Viktor Fischl's *Kuropění* (see p. 16): while Fishl's solitary village doctor can live in peace (presumably in a politically quiet country), adoring the beauty and serenity of his pet cock, Křesadlo's practitioner doctor, working among peasants and Romas in the Czech border country after the war, is too busy, too worried about his responsibilities and frustrated by the government bureaucracy and vigilance, to "go lyrical" about his blind pet cock. *Calle Neruda* (Prague, Ivo Železný, 1994) presents a caricature of the life after 1989 when the Czechs' enthusiasm for anything western was felt: the inhabitants of the famous Neruda Street in Prague adopted Spanish ways.

Yet, behind all the shocks Křesadlo prepared for his readers by the open exposure of sexual perversities, the voice of a moralist can be heard.

## *Mrchopěvci*

Jan Křesadlo was already in his late fifties when he wrote his first novel, "The Funeral Singers"; he did so in the amazingly short time of only three weeks. The writer and publisher Josef Škvorecký, to whom the author submitted it for publication, immediately recognized the originality of the work, which was soon awarded the Egon Hostovský literary prize. Křesadlo's unusual creative freedom of thought and expression shocked some critics and readers; in fact, the cover of a later edition warns that the book is not suitable for puritans. Although there was no shortage of contemporary "oversexed" novels by reputable writers, Křesadlo's gothic horror story certainly came as a surprise.

Literary *débuts* tend to contain more autobiographical details and are also more spontaneous than later works by their creators; this is the case with "The Funeral Singers". Its author, an outspoken freedom lover who did not give in easily, had to live first under the Nazi and then under the communist yoke, being persecuted by both for his "bourgeois origin" and for his refusal to bend to them. Yet, this incredibly talented polymath's employment in the department for sexual deviations at the Faculty of Psychiatry in Prague could hardly fail to influence his artistic imagination. That is how he could create the bizarre milieu full of horrors, disgust, intimidation, fear and violence, which humiliate the hero Zderad and lead him to despair. During the hard Stalinist era (1948–53) the protagonist earns his living as a member of a funeral singers' group, but falls victim to a communist exponent collaborating with the secret police, a homosexual pervert who exploits him by intimidation. He possesses Zderad's poem (in old Greek!) ridiculing Stalin, so incriminating its author. Knowing only too well about the cruel ways the régime treated his father (who died in prison) and the suspicious abduction of his sister, he realizes that his degrading, though sheltered, job won't save him; it is inevitable for him to submit to the sadist monster who coaxes him to join him periodically in a disused cemetery crypt. The place becomes a chamber of horror for Zderad; horror of which the reader is well aware, although in this novel Křesadlo modestly avoids explicit description, as he is "writing an essentially decent story".

If only Zderad could get back his incriminating poem! He tries to do so by a farcical burglary organized by a group of skilful gypsy "professionals", while the monster is on holiday with his family. A lot of property is taken from the palatial place, but, alas, no poem. By now the hero has found that his torturer is a former catholic priest, now an enthusiastic university lecturer in marxism – omnipotent within the régime, who has done a lot of harm to several people.

Zderad's self-respect is very low: feeling like a prostitute and now even as a burglar, he despairs; the only way to get out of the pervert's power seems to him to be suicide, killing his wife and child first. However, the bitter cup overflows and gives the hero strength to resist when the pervert requires involvement of Zderad's wife (she, too, had already been sexually exploited by another high-ranking communist). The couple succeed in killing the monster and bury his body under the crypt. He is never found there, but it is safer for the liberated couple to take refuge abroad. The befriended gypsies help again – dropping them from the bridge onto a passing boat, like pieces of cargo. This kind of ending seems absurd and farcical, but it is quite consistent with the gypsies' skill to outwit, perhaps even to take revenge, on the hated overlords. If the escape looks implausible, many real refugees from the communist régime can testify to the credibility of such or similar ways of escape, as they themselves have been through the experience.

We may take the novel's villain and his world as a symbol of the corruption and moral degeneration of the communist régime, as well as the author's protest against them. If the original subject came rather easily to him from his profession, his extraordinary imagination (especially to invent horror) contributed to the creation of grotesque scenes, gruesome details and a narrative full of tension, like in a detective story – for example, the bizarre action leading to the murder in the crypt – but other scenes are savoured with humour and parody. The author can be cynical, too, when he wishes to show his moral aversion towards any kind of brutality and force. He addresses the reader in a familiar way and is constantly in contact with him; he treats him with pleasant passages about music, a subject which seems to have a purifying effect in the murky atmosphere. Only, it is a pity that the other funeral singers did not take a more prominent part in the novel.

As for style, Křesadlo is a born narrator as well as linguist: he delights in word-play, using phrases from various languages, be it Greek, mutilated Slovak, Hungarian, German, gypsy slang – he can also characterize a country priest by his speech. This kind of cheerful playfulness may look exhibitionist at times, but its humorously animating function in the otherwise dark novel is most beneficial.

# EDA KRISEOVÁ

## Václav Havel
### Brno, Atlantis, 1991

EDA KRISEOVÁ (born 1940) is a fiction writer as well as a journalist. She studied at the school of journalism (part of the Faculty of Philosophy at the Charles University in Prague) and worked first as a reporter. Since she joined the dissidents, she could publish only abroad or in *samizdat.* After the election of Václav Havel as the President of the free Czechoslovakia she became one of his advisers (1990–1992).

Her writings oscilate between the realistic documentary and the dreamy fictional, almost bizarre. Already her early collections of short stories, unusually entitled as *Křížová cesta kočárového kočího* ("The Calvary of a Horse-carriage Coachman", Toronto, 1979) and *Klíční kůstka netopýra* ("The Collarbone of a Bat", Toronto, 1982) signal the promising potential of a writer gifted with great imagination and fine sensitivity. The first presents pitiful characters, damaged in various ways by the totalitarian régime; they are doomed to life in a mental care home. For all their "deviations" they appear almost more normal than the robot-like society outside – but the stories stress their human plight more than the idea of a political protest.

In the other collection, "good old days" are numbered as people get obsessed by consumerism (in spite of the shortages in the shops) and greed for property, but the longest, eponymous and rather different novelette towers in this collection above all by its artistic excellence. The heroine, Eusika, a shy, withdrawn young adult, believes that the amulet, a dried collarbone of a bat, will bring back her beloved Gabriel who had left her because she was scared to give him the ultimate, physical, proof of her love. The analysis of Eusika's inner struggle with herself results in a subtle poem in prose, full of beautiful imagery with fitting rhythm. It is charged with eroticism as the heroine longs to be loved, yet is apprehensive to face the step into the fully adult world which she would enter by losing her virginity. Colourful descriptions of nature's beauties intensify the tension in the dreamy atmosphere of Eusika's search for her Gabriel, her angel.

In the collection of short stories *Arboretum* (Cologne, 1987), Kriseová delves into the deep roots of human existence, love and death; in fact, as in her other stories, here, too, all kinds of love play their part, in a web of relations and their mysteries. After 1989 she published two novels, *Kočičí životy* ("Cat Lives") and *Misericordia*.

The more realistic-documentary line of Kriseová's work is represented by the voluminous, fictional biography, almost a legend, *Václav Havel*, written under the spell of the euphoria of the Velvet Revolution, 1989. Her views on contemporary global civilization appeared in her book *Čísi svět* ("Anybody's World", 2000), inspired by Kriseová's journey to India.

## *Václav Havel*

The dissident movement in communist Czechoslovakia has brought together people of like minds and of great courage; they have learnt to know each other well, and it is only natural that one of them should compile the biography of Václav Havel, the acknowledged leader of the movement and eventually President of the new republic. Unfortunately, Kriseová does not seem to have been the best choice for the task, which was carried out by her in haste. Her skill as a fiction writer misled her into a *biographie romancée;* genre-wise, a kind of hybrid wherein the characteristics of a memoir prevail.

Chronologically, there is a certain amount of unnecessary chaos in the book; the flashbacks, which might have been used successfully in a novel, only underline the lack of discipline and organization here, sometimes overshadowing vital factual new information: for example, the section about King Jiří College, which Havel attended in his early teens, follows the chapter wherein the reader meets him at age twenty-nine, as an editor of the journal *Tvář*. Other such jumps, unwelcome in a biography, abound. Two endearing little stories from Havel's College years may be read with pleasure, whereas others, meant to have the same effect, misfire; the friendship between author and subject, which Kriseová claims throughout the book, leads to a familiarity that is unsuitable in a biography of a man who has become a respected and loved head of state.

In Czechoslovakia the biography received little acclaim. The President's "authorization" that the book is "(Kriseová's) own view of his life and work" sounds diplomatically noncommittal, and in Prečan's view in *Lidové noviny* of 15 August 1991 the cons outweigh the pros. Perhaps the most devastating criticism comes from the pen of Sergej Machonin, a former dissident who supplied some material for Kriseová. One cannot help comparing (as Machonin does) the present book with Karel Čapek's excellent three-volume biography of President T. G. Masaryk, the writing of which was preceded by "about nine years of inquiring, contemplating, remembering and – silence". The blunder of Kriseová's familiarity Machonin measures mercilessly against Čapek's sensitivity and tact: how would it sound, say, if Masaryk and Čapek addressed each other as "Tommy" and "Charlie"?

Knowing so many people close to Havel, Kriseová had much first-hand material within reach. She also had the Havel family archives to consult, and, last but not least, all the works by Havel himself; sadly, this last and most important source has not been given much attention. The author's meditations interspersed in the book sound pretentiously authoritative, concealing a lack of true scholarship. Ambiguities and inaccuracies provoke questions for which the reader will not find answers either in the text or in the notes attached.

Still, the book is not without merit. It includes several hitherto unknown facts, and the picture of the past work and collaboration of the dissidents is interesting, vivid, and often amusing in the black-humour way Havel likes. Many individuals play their parts in the book well (though Mrs. Olga Havel appears too casual), but their contribution does not always focus on Havel's leading role. Thus Havel's pen portrait remains hazy among events which happened to

Kriseová herself. The photograph section of the book is the best part of it.

In English

*Václav Havel,* Caleb Crain, trans., London, St. Martin's Press, 1993.

# MILAN KUNDERA

## *Žert*
## ("The Joke")
### Prague, Československý spisovatel, 1967

MILAN KUNDERA was born in 1929. His father, Ludvík Kundera, was a renowned musicologist and concert pianist. Milan, too, played the piano from his childhood and music later influenced his writings significantly. He started studying literature and aesthetics at the Charles University at Prague, but changed his subject after two semesters for cinematography at the Film Faculty. In 1964 he was appointed at this institution as lecturer in world literature. Kundera joined the communist party in 1948, but was expelled two years later; he was accepted again in 1956, only to lose his membership in 1970. He moved to France in 1975 and was deprived of his Czech citizenship four years later.

Kundera has entered literature as a poet, playwright and essayist, but the form of novel suited him best. He excelled with his first, *Žert* ("The Joke"), which seems to me still to be his most outstanding. It was preceded by three volumes of short stories, *Směšné lásky* (Prague, 1963, 1965, 1968, in one volume in 1970; "Laughable Loves"). They already signal some characteristics of Kundera's subsequent novels, a kind of melancholy in the lives of contemporary people; characters in situations where they fail in their actions through their own folly or unexpected circumstances; his dislike of superficiality and kitsch in life and art; a slightly frivolous approach to the art of writing; innocent, light phrases causing painful, grotesque twists in the lives of people in the communist-governed society.

Some of Kundera's novels could be published in Czechoslovakia, but most of them came out abroad, in quick succession: *Život je jinde* (first published in French translation, 1973; in Czech: Toronto, Sixty-Eight Publishers, 1979; "Life is Elsewhere", New York and London, 1974, 1986); *Valčík na rozloučenou* (first in French, 1976; in Czech: Toronto, Sixty-Eight Publishers, 1979; "The Farewell Party", New York, 1976; London, 1977); *Kniha smíchu a zapomnění* (first in French, 1979; in Czech: Toronto, Sixty-Eight Publishers, 1981, "The Book of Laughter and Forgetting", London, 1996); *Nesnesitelná lehkost bytí* (first in French, 1984; in Czech: Toronto, Sixty-Eight Publishers, 1985; "The Unbearable Lightness of Being", New York, 1984, London, 1984); *Nesmrtelnost* (first in French, 1990; in Czech: Brno, Atlantis, 1993). "Immortality" (London, 1991) was the last novel to be published in French translation; from now on Kundera wrote in French direct and, instead of in Czech as might be expected, his following three novels came out in English translations: *La lenteur* (1995; "Slowness", London and Boston, 1996), *L' identité* (1997, "Identity" , New York, 1998), *L'ignorance* (2003, "Ignorance", New York, 2002, London, 2003).

Kundera elucidates his ideas and ways of writing in the book of essays, *L' art du roman* (Paris, 1986; "The Art of the Novel", trans. Linda Asher, New York, Grove Press, 1988; London, Faber and Faber, 1988), where he also discusses European literary traditions, referring to, among others, Miguel de Cervantes, Gustave Flaubert, Robert Musil, Hermann Broch, Thomas Mann, Franz Kafka.

## The Joke

There is something of the author himself in his youthful protagonist, the student Ludvík Jahn, an enthusiastic communist at the time of the communist *coup d'état* in Czechoslovakia in 1948; however, Ludvík's joking, mocking sense of humour clashes with the rigid solemnity in which marxism is officially shrouded. His promising career is turned upside-down after he has sent a card to his all-too-serious girlfriend Marketa, now outside Prague, attending a course in party training. Ludvík's lighthearted outburst "optimism is the opium of the people! A healthy atmosphere stinks of stupidity! Long live Trotsky!" is taken seriously not only by

Marketa, but even more so by the communist students' council who dictate their consequential verdict.

Expelled from the communist party as well as the university, the only way open to him now is his national service which, in his case, means that he has to join the army's "black corps" of "unreliable" people who have to work in the coal mines in Ostrava. During several years of hardship, being treated inhumanely and isolated spiritually, Ludvík cannot help thinking of revenge on those who have ruined his life – even if, eventually, he is rehabilitated and can work where his abilities aren't wasted.

Marketa, actually, did not betray him when his life was being wrecked by politics; helplessly, she only accepted the inevitable. But the grudge Ludvík held against his former colleague Pavel Zemánek remained fresh in his heart and mind. When chance brings him close to Zemánek's wife, Helena, he exploits her tender feelings she declares for him, by sexually abusing her – only to find that time has progressed and the situation changed: Zemánek's political views have now become more liberal and he no longer loves Helena, even seeks divorce from her. Ludvík's revenge on him through Helena turns very convenient for the antagonist.

Then Ludvík meets another person from his past, a gentle Christian believer Kostka, whom he had done a good turn when Kostka found himself in a similar crisis to Ludvík's. He could revive some spiritual values in Ludvík's damaged soul, but the latter suffers pain when Kostka reveals to him the secret of Lucie, the guileless, modest girl whose love meant so much for Ludvík during his coalmining period, but who vanished when he claimed his right to have sex with her.

When Ludvík visits his native town in Moravia, near the Slovak border, he deplores the general decline, with all the drabness and general neglect, as well as poor services to the public. He acknowledges the tone of resignation in his childhood friend Jaroslav, a guardian of good old values, which include folk festivals, now being performed without any spontaneity and pleasure in its art. According to Kundera, he himself admired the colourful "Ride of the Kings", celebrated in the area; the event plays an important part in the book, illustrating the festival vividly, but also implying Kundera's regret over the folklore art being censored by insensitive officialdom. Ludvík joins the band with his clarinet, but Jaroslav becomes a tragic hero of this final part of the novel. As he plays his violin, he suffers a heart attack and Ludvík can only witness his friend's transfer to hospital.

These four narrators build up the novel which, in fact, has no single, definite plot. This is no disadvantage, as it gives this innovative structure its polyphonic character: instead of a plot, there are themes as in music. Ludvík represents the theme of the joke; Helena the one of revenge; Lucie the theme of forgetting (for all his affection Ludvík had for her, he fails to recognize her at their chance meeting years later); Kostka the theme of Christian moral stability; Jaroslav the theme of the man in relation to history and good tradition in art and life. As in music, the pace of the actions changes according to their importance, but, as the themes mutually permeate, they merge at the end into an impressive fugue. At the same time, if we take the single narrations as monologues, the characters come out as fully drawn, seen from several perspectives, Ludvík the most prominent among them.

Considering Kundera's later novels, one can see already in *The Joke* the author's concern in distinguishing true love from mere sex. Ludvík loves Lucie even without sex, while his sex without love with Helena appears here in all its brutality. In his later novels sex seems increasingly more important to Kundera; it inclines almost to pornography. He also likes to stress his ideas by passages in an essayistic style; while they flow freely and naturally in the text of *The Joke* (on music), they later tend to prevail over the action, becoming a mannerism which distracts rather than illuminates.

*The Joke* is written very well and one can fully agree with Louis Aragon that it is "one of the greatest novels of the century". Would he say the same about Kundera's later novels? Actually, the latest three, *Slowness, Identity, Ignorance,* were originally written in French and Kundera considers himself a French novelist ever since. His Czech compatriots may no longer read anything by him in his first language.

In English

*The Farewell Party*, Peter Kussi, trans., New York, A. Knopf, 1976; London, John Murray, 1977.

*The Unbearable Lightness of Being*, Michael Heim, trans., New York, Harper and Row, 1984; London, Faber and Faber, 1984.

*Life is Elsewhere,* Peter Kussi, trans., New York, A. Knopf, 1974, London, Faber and Faber, 1986.

*Laughable Loves,* Susanne Rappaport, trans., New York, A. Knopf, 1974, London, Faber and Faber, 1991.

*Immortality,* Peter Kussi, trans., London, Faber and Faber, 1991.

*The Book of Laughter and Forgetting*, Aaron Asher, trans., London, Faber and Faber, 1996.

*Slowness,* Linda Asher, trans., London and Boston, Faber and Faber, 1996.

*Identity,* Linda Asher, trans., New York, Harper Flamingo, 1998.

*The Art of the Novel,* Linda Asher, trans., New York, Grove Press, 1986, London, Faber and Faber, 1988.

# ARNOŠT LUSTIG

## *Dita Saxová*
Toronto, Sixty-Eight Publishers, 1982

## *Porgess* (in *Velká trojka*)
("The Great Three")
Prague, Galaxie, 1991

ARNOŠT LUSTIG (born 1926), son of a Prague retailer, was expelled from his school because of his Jewish origin. In 1942 he was sent to the ghetto in Terezín and transported to the concentration camps in Auschwitz and then Buchenwald, respectively. Shortly before the end of the war he managed to escape from the death transport for Dachau. After the liberation he studied journalism at the Faculty of Political and Social Studies in Prague, but started working as a journalist before he finished his studies in 1954. He contributed to many important periodicals in Prague as well as in his exile for which he left in 1968. He lived first in Italy, Israel and Yugoslavia before settling more permanently in the United States in 1970. There he held positions at the universities of Iowa, Nebraska and Washington D.C., at the last one, finally, as Professor of Literature and Film.

His work is concerned almost exclusively with Jewish themes, with characters finding themselves in life-threatening or morally crucial situations, full of fear, horror and danger; situations out of which some of them emerge morally or spiritually transformed. Lustig wrote mostly shorter pieces, novelettes and short stories prevailing; the latter came out in various collections so that the stories overlap, but each of them has its individual value. Many have also appeared in English translations.

In the first two collections, *Noc a naděje* ("Night and Hope", 1957), and *Démanty noci* ("Diamonds of the Night", 1958), Lustig writes about the most vulnerable – children and elderly people – exposed to cruelty in extreme situations in the concentration camps. In two more extensive works, *Dita Saxová* ("Dita Sax", 1962), and *Můj známý Vili Feld* ("My Acquaintance Vili Feld", 1961), Lustig concentrates on individual dominant characters, people whose lives were permanently marked by the traumatic experience of war, so that their difficulties in adjusting later to normal life leads to tragedy. The theme of humiliation to which Nazi camp masters subjected their victims dominates in *Modlitba za Kateřinu Horowitzovou* ("A Prayer for Kateřina Horowitz", 1964); in *Z deníku sedmnáctileté Perly Sch . . .* (Toronto, Sixty-Eight Publishers, 1979; "The Unloved", 1985) the life of the seventeen-year-old heroine is destroyed by the forced prostitution. Two publications came out first in English: *Darkness Casts no Shadow* (Washington D.C., 1976, "Tma Nemá Stín") and *Indecent Dreams* (Evanston, 1988, "Neslušné Sny). *Krásné zelené oči* ("Lovely Green Eyes) came out in Czech in 2000, translated into English the following year.

Life in the US did not inspire Lustig to write about it – on the contrary, even as late as in the nineties he turned back to the past – the war, the Jews, the Nazis – in *Porgess* (1989, 1991), *Colette, dívka z Antverp* ("Colette, a Girl from Antwerp", 1992), *Tanga, dívka z Hamburku* ("Tanga, a Girl from Hamburg", 1993) and *Kamarádi* ("Friends", 1995).

## Dita Saxová

The heroine , Dita Sax, represents in this novel the type of young Jewish people who had survived the Holocaust, having entered the hell as children and left it after the liberation, still "too young to be left on their own and too grown-up to allow anyone to look after them" (p. 250). Dita, aged eighteen, lost both her parents in the gas chambers of the Nazi camps and experienced horrors which have marked her for the rest of her life. She now lives in a home for orphaned Jewish girls, is employed in the archives of the Jewish community, studies arts and crafts and socializes with other girls in the home, as well as with the boys from a similar, nearby home. She is attractive and would, in normal circumstances, easily find a loving partner for a happy life; yet, she seems to be wavering, undecided, not knowing how to do any better. Most of the novel is filled with Dita's thoughts, a kind of interior monologue, while the other characters play only a minor part; in fact, externally, the whole story is very simple: the young man for whom she feels some inclination is uncertain of himself in a similar way to Dita and leaves for abroad before any deeper relationship can develop. Dita's other admirers don't seem to count; towards the end of the story her dull life is brightened up by a stay in Grindelwald as a carer for orphaned Jewish children.

This could be an opportunity for Dita to find some purpose for her life, looking after the young, abandoned creatures, to make their lives worth living as well as her own, but, no, the reader never sees them in Dita's company or even in her thoughts; they are mentioned in the book only to indicate that the scene has changed from Prague to Switzerland. Dita admires the beauty of the Alps and keeps on dreaming about the life she would like to lead, but her mind wanders back to the past. Even a fairly pleasant party where she met and formed some sort of relationship with two Swiss brothers, Peter and Paul, did not make any impression on her. Taking leave of them after the party in the middle of the night, she walks and walks on the snow-clad mountain path and falls to her death in a ravine. Suicide or accident? There was no suicide in Dita's mind before she set out for her walk: why did she go out on her own, on this night, in Switzerland, in 1948? Who knows what dark powers were still lingering in the subconscious of her injured mind?

Lustig achieves a great power of expression by the intensity of his style. He writes in short sentences, just as the human mind tends to flicker from one thought to another, and they frequently conclude in unusual metaphors: talking about the force of fate, Lisa says to Dita: "Perhaps one can't deceive one's fate. Don't we say that what fate outlines in black, not even the sun can whiten?" Saying this, . . . "she sounded . . . as if the owl would sing and the nightingale weep"(p. 211). Dita's belief that "life isn't what we want, but what we have" (p. 97) may contain some kind of reconciliation and hope, but the image of the singing owl and the weeping nightingale seem to indicate the dark side in her mind and may even justify her suicide.

## Porgess (in Velká trojka), Prague, Galaxie, 1991

Taking Lustig's work as a whole, one can say that, in general, his inspiration lies in the horrors of the Holocaust and the scars left on the lives of those who have survived. Among his characters he feels most strongly for adolescent girls who were forced to prostitution in order to survive; some of his books entitled by a girl's name indicate that; but his men suffered, too: *Porgess* is an example. The story came out as one of three longer short stories, written by Arnošt Lustig (*Porgess,* 1989), Milan Kundera (*Ztracené dopisy* II, 1978, "Lost Letters II") and Josef Škvorecký (*Trip do Česka,* 1982, "A Trip to Czecho"), respectively. While Škvorecký's story is hilarious, abounding in extravagant humour, Kundera's expresses sadness and frustration and Lustig's deals again with consequences of the Holocaust.

Porgess, a handsome young Jew, survives the Nazi persecution, though just barely; he manages to escape from the death transport at the end of the war only to remain paralyzed for life by the guard's bullets. His narrator friend, feeling almost guilty for his own good health, continues to support him through his visits; their reminiscences and discussions of contemporary matters weave the story out of a complicated set of flashbacks and present events into a clear pattern. Trivial as their talks may sound, they express great human truths through Lustig's skilful use of irony. The healthy narrator's consideration of the patient's predicament directs his speech – an accomplishment of great authorial subtlety.

In English

*Diamonds of the Night*, Iris Urwin, trans., Prague, Artia, 1962. Jeanne Němcová, trans., London, Quartet, 1989.

*Night and Hope,* George Theiner, trans., Washington, Inscape, 1976; London, Quartet, 1989.

*Darkness Casts no Shadow,* Jeanne Němcová, trans., Washington, Inscape, 1976, London, Quartet, 1989.

*A Prayer fir Katerina Horowitzová*, Jeanne Němcová, trans., London, Quartet, 1990.

*Indecent Dreams,* Iris Urwin-Levit, Věra Bořkovec, Paul Wilson, trans., Evanston, Ill., Northwestern University Press, 1990.

*Dita Saxová,* Jeanne Němcová, trans., London, Quartet, 1994.

*Children of the Holocaust,* Jeanne Němcová, George Theiner, trans., Evanston, Ill., Northwestern University Press, 1995.

*Lovely Green Eyes,* Ewald Osers, trans., London, Harvill, 2001, Vintage, 2005.

# VLADIMÍR NEFF

*Sňatky z rozumu*
("Marriages of Convenience", 1957)

*Císařské fialky*
("Emperor Violets", 1958)

*Zlá krev*
("Ill Blood", 1959)

*Veselá vdova*
("Merry Widow", 1961)

*Královský vozataj*
("King's Charioteer", 1963)

Collected edition, Prague, Československý spisovatel, 1965

VLADIMÍR NEFF (1909–1983) was born in Prague in a merchant family. After his grammar school and commercial academy studies in Prague, he studied commerce in Geneva. He spent his "gap year" in Vienna and Bremen, after which he became an editor in the publishing house Melantrich. He contributed to many leading periodicals and became a professional writer in 1939.

Neff started his career with the publication of short stories (*Nesnáze Ibrahima Skály*; "Ibrahim Skála's Difficulties", 1933; *Papírové panoptikum*; "A Paper Panorama", 1934), but already in his early novel *Malý velikán* ("A Little Genius", 1933) he succeeded very well in the analysis of a child's mind, the theme which he developed even better in the following novel, *Třináctá komnata*

("The Thirteenth Chamber", 1934): here he drew the emotional and moral growth of two young people very skilfully. With the two protagonists, Kost'a and Blanka, entangled in a detective theme and set into the charming part of Prague, the picturesque little island of Kampa, this novel could be compared with Henry James' *What Maisie Knew*. It may well be the best that Neff ever wrote. It was followed by a short novel, also set in the Kampa, *Marie a zahradník* ("Marie and the Gardener", 1945), full of passion – erotic and religious.

After the war Neff turned to history for inspiration. Interested in genealogy, he became quite prolific in the creation of historical novels. *Srpnovští páni* ("The Masters of Srpnov", 1953), with the stress on human freedom and predestination, it is set in the reign of the last Přemislides and the following, of John of Luxembourg (approx. 1293–1318). It shows already the author's very conscientious study of history, but, at the same time, his narrative style tends to suffer from lengthy passages of historical, economic or religious argument: apart from novels, Neff has also published *Filosofický slovník pro samouky neboli Antigorgias* ("A Dictionary of Philosophy, Self-taught", 1948).

Genealogy, combined with Neff's family background, inspired the sequel of five novels, developing the theme of capable, enterprising and successful people whose children, instead of doing better than their parents, turn out to be rather mediocre and producing offspring of weak, unreliable individuals. Actually, this theme interested Neff even earlier, in the novels *Dva u stolu* ("Two at the Table", 1937) and *Vyhnaní z ráje* ("Expelled from Paradise", 1939). Yet, the quintet, *Sňatky z rozumu, Císařské fialky, Zlá krev, Veselá vdova, Královský vozataj*, must be considered his most elaborate novel chronicle. The sequel came out as one collection in 1965 and was followed by *Trampoty pana Humbla* ("Mr. Humbl's Misfortunes", 1967), a novel dealing with a crook, similar to Hrabal's protagonist of his novel *I Served the King of England*. Afterwards, a trilogy came out, a parody on the 17th century history, *Královny nemají nohy* ("Queens Have no Legs", 1973), *Prsten Borgiů* ("The Ring of the Borgias", 1975), *Krásná čarodějka* ("A Beautiful Enchantress", 1980). Neff's last novel, *Roucho pana de Balzac* ("Mr. de Balzac's Gown", 1981), is a comic extravaganza about an imaginary gift of Balzac's garment which he wore when writing his novels, to a young, insignificant writer.

## Sňatky z rozumu, Císařské fialky, Zlá krev, Veselá vdova, Královský vozataj

Turning to history for inspiration was a clever idea of Czech writers, restricted by the totalitarian ideology in their choice of their subjects and the treatment of them; even if they used irony in their dealing with history, they could not be easily accused of "wrong" views. When Neff was writing his five-part saga, private retailers and department stores had been appropriated by the state for a long time (since 1948), but the memories of his merchant forebears, as well as his own experience during the time of the free Czechoslovak Republic, could be well used for historical novels, containing also threads of autobiography. The saga covers the time-span of approximately one hundred years, up to the end of Second World War.

Two main protagonists, businessmen of a different kind, tower above any other character in the multitude of them: the genteel, sensible, honest and patriotic Jan Born, and the disillusioned, hard-working, stubborn Martin Nedobyl. The powerful introductory sentence of the first book signals what happened to the latter: "One cannot ever get used to any wrong done to one, whether 'one' means a nation, a city, an individual. One cannot get used to it; only, in time, the anger gets weaker, smaller, sour; it gets silent and sad, slouched and pointless." Cruelly treated in the then Austrian army and wrongly accused later in a Catholic seminary, Nedobyl becomes hard, even rough and selfish when he takes over his father's stage-coach and removal business; stubbornly he works hard, determined to get rich. The idealist Born cherishes the hope to open a large, "Slavonic" department store in the centre of Prague; conveniently marrying the daughter of a rich widow, his dream of enlarging what he already possessed looked increasingly like becoming a reality. Nedobyl marries the (still young enough) widow herself – a much more lively and energetic person than her daughter. With her support and talent for business, his trade flourishes; he can now buy lots of land for speculation and become increasingly richer and more powerful.

Born's marriage fails, but he does not lose his spirit and trust in his intelligent enterprise. The building of new railway lines makes it easier for him to introduce new imported products and enlarge his store. More customers and the developments in banking increase the capital in Czech hands, giving the nation a better security and freedom from the German element which surrounded and suppressed them. Born's patriotic ideals place him in a position of strength in the sequel, while Nedobyl appears as a ruthless speculator, hated by his competing neighbours and his own employees, especially Karel Pecold who, in his poverty, fails to notice that Nedobyl wishes to treat him fairly, even kindly. The resentful Pecold represents the third family line, the lower class, whose mistrust towards their employers leads to strikes and demonstrations.

As the number of characters grows, some of them have to be removed from the scene: Neff does not hesitate to "kill them off" suddenly, so that the story can take a new direction and new episodes can follow. So, the unfaithful wife of Jan Born and her cheerful mother, happily married to Nedobyl, perish in a train crash (one actually happened in 1868 on the Prague–Pilsen line); Born's honest effort to give the best education to his orphaned son Míša leads to the boy's suicide after his mind has been twisted by one of his teachers, Míša's role model, who trained him to become, discreetly, an Austrian informer as he was himself. In this touching episode the Czech patriotic and concerned father never finds out, nor even suspects, the reason for Míša's suicide; it is presented to the reader with great sensitivity.

Mutual love between Jan Born and the beautiful, elegant Hana, daughter of a lawyer, leads to a happy marriage; the business prospers and Hana shines in the splendid parties she organizes at their home to gather the Czech cultural élite. Real historical personalities of all cultural circles flit past (Antonín Dvořák is illustrated, accompanying on the piano his *Moravian Duets*, sung by Hana and her sister) – just to remind the reader of the period of the action. Even Nedobyl visits here occasionally (let's not forget that their first marriages made Born Nedobyl's son-in-law) – and he eventually finds his second wife there, a young, delicate, very musical, intelligent and well educated Marie. She is practically forced to accept Nedobyl: her widowed father, a "Privatdozent" in philosophy (who was qualified and could lecture at universities, but without being paid), found himself stranded after the family capital was finally spent. The reader follows with horror Marie's sacrifice; she serves the ungainly, coarse, cheese-paring but fair provider for herself and her father obediently, bearing him four gifted children – but she becomes "the merry widow" of the fourth book of the saga after his death. No, she does not indulge in affairs with men; rich as she now is, she enjoys buying and using a country villa, good clothes and spending without limit on the education of her children.

As the families of the Borns, Nedobyls and Pecolds grow and branch off, the saga becomes thickly populated. Each character has a story – Neff's imagination seems inexhaustible in this respect; but he realizes that human life is unpredictable, ups and downs intermingle. Neither of the Borns' two sons from the second marriage show their parents' nobility and the father's business talent; Marie's musically unusually gifted eldest son dies young; his brother's promising career as a great opera singer ends suddenly by his stagefright (he becomes a good painter, taught by the famous Jan Slavíček, but is not earning enough to be independent); one of the third-generation Nedobyls, Albert, a genial construction engineer, dies having crashed his car; the young Cyril Born (grandson of Jan and Hana) escapes from the family business to become an editor in a large publishing house – Neff describing scenes from there, so familiar to him, with a good deal of irony; one of the young Pecolds disgraces the "revolutionary" family by joining a troupe of travelling actors.

The stories in the sequel are well linked by a narrator as well as their setting against the background of history. Not only Central Europe: events in the whole world influence the lives of his characters. Could Neff be considered as a Czech parallel to John Galsworthy? Yes, in the sense that both their sagas are founded on money; both writers have shown a penetrating knowledge of human nature; both used irony to express their feelings, both created interesting and credible studies of character, virile, robust, but also weak individuals. But their use of the background differs: Galsworthy was not so much concerned about history itself, while Neff's aim was to write purely historical novels. Yet, "what happens around" cannot be disregarded, even if long descriptions can slacken the stream of the narration: where Galsworthy uses passages of gentle mood contemplation, Neff gives a full, sometimes even boring, lessons in history.

Neff certainly took great pains to verify historical facts; his poetic imagination created stories which could have actually happened. He himself declared (in an interview, 30 July 1980, *Nové knihy*) that, although he cannot prove to historians that his historical fancies are true, they themselves cannot prove that they could not happen.

# JAN OTČENÁŠEK

## *Kulhavý Orfeus*
### ("The Limping Orpheus")
Prague, Československý spisovatel, 1964

Jan Otčenášek (1924–1979), born in a Prague working-class suburb (Žižkov), studied at a school of commerce. Under the Nazi rule he, too, like most Czech young men born in 1924, had to join the *Totaleinsatz*, to work in a munitions factory during the final year of the war. It was also during this period that he became a member of an illegal resistance group of young people (cf. "The Limping Orpheus"). After the war he worked as editor in the broadcasting corporation and later (1956–60) as the secretary of the Writers' Union. After 1960, as a successful professional writer, he produced works, several of which were dramatized or filmed.

His novel *Plným krokem* ("Full Step Forward", 1952) was hailed as progressive ("constructive" in the communist technical terminology), as was his more extensive novel *Občan Brych* ("Citizen Brych", 1955) in which the hero, wavering between the idea of emigrating or staying in the communist-run state, favours the latter. Otčenášek's most popular novel *Romeo, Julie a tma* ("Romeo, Juliet and the Darkness") came out in 1958, a well written record of the Prague life of horrors after the *Reichsprotektor* Heidrich's assassination – a subject strongly reminiscent of *Anne Frank's Diary*. Autobiographical features can be traced in *Kulhavý Orfeus* and even more so in *Pokušení Katarina* ("The Tempting Island of Katarina") which remained unfinished and was published posthumously in 1984.

## *Kulhavý Orfeus*

The book consists of several plots constructed around the single characters, linked to form a harmonious pattern by their mutual acquaintance made in the factory where they had been sent to work within the *Totaleinsatz* scheme, and where also the group, The Orpheus, was formed. Otčenášek is a good narrator with a fine sense for depicting the atmosphere of the time, which is here powerfully represented.

The characters move rather aimlessly, vegetating and waiting to start new lives after the end of the war; their unsuccessful attempts to join some efficient underground movement (hence the title "The Limping Orpheus") take a considerable part of the novel. The main, finely drawn character, Honza, wins sympathy when his love affair, at first a bright ray in the dense atmosphere, ends with his discovery that his beloved Blanka has sacrificed herself as mistress to an influential Nazi officer in order to save the life of her imprisoned brother; the uncertainty of life is reflected in Dušan, a suicide, to whom nature and good luck have been very generous, so that his suicide emerges as an expression of perfect personal freedom in the occupied country. Bacil, as a character, has some humorous touches, but the overdrawn story of Vojta, a haloed working-class young man, is a disturbing element in the pattern of the book. Wild, disgusting scenes at parties held by the "bourgeois" people (to whom belongs also Vojta's dearly loved, though only nominal, wife Alena) are described in great detail and Vojta suffers in silence the humiliation of being beaten up by Alena's lover and tolerating her illegitimate pregnancy; his blind love is almost incurable and he has to find Alena in bed with her lover to be brought back to his senses. In this part, instead of the intended thrill, the author achieves the contrary effect which can be only partly outweighed by more successful episodes: for example, the extremely powerful climax of Blanka's affair in which she murders the perfidious Nazi officer who exploited her when her brother was already dead.

People who lived through this period in Bohemia or Moravia may be ready to find excuses for all the eccentricities of the characters' behaviour, but their refuge in sex as the panacea for relieving mental pain and distress doesn't sound convincing.

As far as language is concerned, Otčenášek's expression spreads on a large scale. The adolescent victims of the *Totaleinsatz* use their rough, spontaneous slang; the factory workers' jargon isn't refined either and the middle-class youth, bored and wasting their time while waiting for the end of the war, also have their characteristic, inelegant language, but there are also serious, fluent discussions of philosophical problems as well as expressions of intense feeling and poetical imagery.

In spite of the skill in linking the episodes of this large-scale novel (the construction of the chapter describing activities on New Year's Eve is particularly interesting) and the evocation of the war atmosphere "The Limping Orpheus" is unlikely to surpass the popularity of Otčenášek's "Romeo, Juliet and the Darkness".

# VLADIMIÍR PÁRAL

## *Soukromá vichřice*
("A Private Storm")
Prague, Mladá fronta, 1966

## *Kniha rozkoší, smíchu a radosti*
("The Book of Delight, Laughter and Pleasure")
Prague, Dialog, 1992

VLADIMÍR PÁRAL was born in 1932 in Prague, the son of an army officer, but spent most of his youth in Brno where he studied chemistry at the Technical University. He finished his studies at the newly founded Faculty of Chemistry and Technology in Pardubice in 1954. As a chemistry research worker he was employed in several industrial institutions in different parts of the country, until he became a professional writer. He travelled widely (Central Asia, Canada, China, Nepal . . . ), lived permanently in Ústí nad Labem (North Bohemia) and later in Prague and Mariánské lázně. Although he tried to avoid being involved in politics, he did not fail to notice the monotony of people's daily routine laid down by the rules of their regular work. Life in the totalitarian state appears in his writings as mechanized, as if people were unable to change anything to make it more varied. Over-mechanized civilization creates stereotyped reality, leading individuals to some kind of alienation. People's emotions suffer, too: love has become mere sex. .

Páral's inspiration lies in the routine mechanization; his style is condensed, telegraphic, full of black humour, parody and linguistic tricks. His early protagonists tend to accept the dreary situation, but those of his later works show some effort to get out of the grey reality and find their proper identity. This can be traced in his quintet, *Veletrh splněných přání* ("A Fair of Fulfilled Wishes", 1964), *Soukromá vichřice* ("A Private Storm", 1966), *Katapult* ("Catapult", 1967), *Milenci a vrazi* ("Lovers and Murderers", 1969), and *Profesionální žena* ("A Professional Woman", 1971, translated into English as *The Four Sonyas*).

In 1973 Páral published *Mladý muž a bílá velryba* ("A Young Man and a White Whale"), a novel with a plot from a chemistry plant whose hero finds at least some pleasure in his work, even if the mechanization cannot be completely eliminated; his *Muka obraznosti* ("The Torture of Imagination", 1980), about a young chemistry engineer starting to work in a factory, but wishing to write as well, derives a lot from his own experiences. After 1989, free from the communist censorship, Páral published *Decameron 2000 aneb Láska v Praze* ("Decameron 2000 or Love in Prague", 1990), about various types of loving; *Kniha rozkoší, smíchu a radosti* ("A Book of Delight, Laughter and Pleasure", 1993), *Play-Girls 1–2* (1994) and his real autobiography, *Profesionální muž* ("A Professional Man", 1995).

## Soukromá vichřice

There can be little doubt that V. Páral is one of the great originators of form in contemporary Czech literature. Striving after novelty, after being "with it", Páral's two first works, "The Fair of Fulfilled Wishes" and "A Private Storm", indicate that the author wished to create a new genre in Czech literature, the sex novel.

Where older novelists tried to solve the emotional problems of their heroes, Páral eliminates them, reducing emotional life to mere sex. His characters, who move like figures on a chessboard, have no such problems: it does not matter with whom one sleeps. Formal marriage still exists, but it does not prevent the men from sleeping with their friends' wives. In fact, the chapter headings, reminding one of chemical formulas, give the impression of an experiment to combine the few elements (i.e., characters) in couples, so as to get as many variations as possible.

In this purely materialistic novel life is mechanical, as if reduced, in its monotony, to units which repeat themselves. Contemporary art, literature and film slightly influence the lives of Páral's characters, but the heaped plates of heavy food and the sexual hedonism overshadow any deeper interest in culture. The characters are dehumanized and degraded to a level which (one hopes) society had not really reached then yet.

According to Páral, the book is "a mere analysis preceding synthesis . . . hatred preceding love". His style, based on the principle of repetition, continually adding to the situations like a moving snowball, is certainly interesting and effective, but as a tool it is hardly strong enough to make a great work of art out of the machine-made material.

## (Vladimír Páral), Kniha rozkoší, smíchu a radosti

A trained scientist and self-taught writer, V. Páral combines the two professions very successfully in his writings. When he began his literary career in the sixties, he impressed Josef Škvorecký so much that he described Páral as one of the brightest stars of contemporary Czech literature. While Škvorecký and other Czech writers were fleeing their country after the Soviet invasion, Páral stayed. As "a magician of fiction who can do with his material absolutely everything he pleases" (Škvorecký), he obviously did not annoy the communist authorities too much, for his works continued to be published in spite of the dreariness of the stereotyped life under communism he described. After almost thirty years of experience, he is generally considered one of the most popular and most erotic of Czech writers.

The world in which the protagonist of *Kniha rozkoší, smíchu a radosti* moves is interesting, though the plot is quite simple: a fifty-five-year-old widowed writer, Bohdan Ipser, contemplates remarriage; but after a few pathetic and ridiculous attempts in which he finds himself overwhelmed by a host of unsuitable candidates, he is swept off his feet by the much younger, beautiful, rather simple, but very sexy Naďa, who has no intention of marrying him. Full of sexual vigour, their exhausting affair does not last long; deserted by Naďa, Bohdan casually accepts the (rather repulsive) advances of his keen, pleasure-seeking female friends, only to realize that, in the end, peace and solitude achieved through yoga bring him the greatest contentment.

But, all is not that simple. The title promises delight first and foremost; for Páral's characters the way to bed is usually very short, and what he calls delight, others may describe as near-pornography. Still, how can one criticize such a great, witty stylist as Páral? As we are reminded of sex all too much now, erotica becomes increasingly boring, yet, Páral always seems able to invent new ways to amuse his readers in need of overcoming their growing sense of sickness, disgust and moral indignation. Rather than laughter, Páral evokes chuckles when he ridicules writers' clubs, formal embassy receptions, business speculations, nudist beaches, television recordings, fashion and beauty contests. However, true laughter comes from the hero himself when he reaches some sort of catharsis through yoga. Under this influence he behaves irrationally in public, laughing aloud at the vanity of human striving and longing. Externally, his actions show signs of mental disintegration or senility; his yoga-induced bliss thus does not prove quite convincing.

Whereas in his earlier novel, *Katapult,* Páral led his disintegrating protagonist into serious accident but not necessarily to his death, his yogi hero clearly dies when he crashes his car. As in his earlier works, here, too, Páral uses the repetition of phrases or situations to achieve the effect of life's regularity or even dreary monotony. In "The Private Storm", for example, fifty-two chickens are consumed every year, one each Sunday. In the later book the protagonist's mistress Diana removes her clothes in exactly the same order each time she undresses for Bohdan; his daughter's speech and her husband's conversation are both reduced to a few repeated phrases; TV producers, editors, and businessmen word their requests for Ipser's contributions in exactly the same way each time they see him. The method is quite effective for the creation of Ipser's world. A Naďa, similar to the one thrown into the hero's arms during his travels in *Katapult*, appears here at Ipser's side on his visit to China; there is also a similar collapse of relationships in the two novels.

The hero himself is quite pathetic. Famous, rich and irresistible to women, he has no will of his own when facing (rather improbably) the numerous women who woo him and disrobe before he can ask them to do this (this is particularly overdone in the case of the beautiful and intelligent Dr. Broncová). What a poor victim he looks among the bitchy legion of women, with Dr. Diana Dittrichová the crudest! It is to Ipser's credit that he remembers his late wife with true affection.

For all these reservations, one can admire Páral's fluent style, witty comments and clever neologisms, as well as his technique of characterization through interior monologue and repetition. Perhaps he can really do with his material anything he pleases.

In English

*Catapult,* William Harkins, trans., Highland Park, New Jersey, Catbird Press, 1989.

*The Four Sonyas,* "A Professional Woman", W. E. Harkins, trans., North Haven, CT, Catbird Press, 1993.

*Lovers and Murderers,* Craig Craven, trans., North Haven, CT, Catbird Press, 2001.

# OTA PAVEL

## *Jak jsem potkal ryby*
Prague, 1972

## *How I Came to know Fish*
Translated by Jindřiška Badal and Robert McDowell,
New York, New Directions, 1991

OTA PAVEL (1930–1973) is the pen name of Otto Popper, author of
fictional articles on sport and of autobiographical memoirs. As a
young boy he witnessed his Jewish father and two of his elder
brothers being taken by the Nazis to concentration camps, while he,
too young, was left at home with his gentile mother. Luckily, the
family was re-united after the war. Ota subsequently became a
member of staff in the broadcasting corporation and editor of two
journals, but his activities were marred by his repeated nervous
breakdowns. Yet, in the periods between treatments he produced his
best works.

His interest in sports inspired his first book, *Dukla mezi mrako-
drapy* ("Dukla among the Skyscrapers",[1] 1969); its great success
encouraged him to go on writing, applying the sportsmen's virtues
to the desired values for life: ambition to achieve the best, but also,
if need be, to accept defeat, undaunted. The sports themes prevail in
*Plná bedna šampaňského* ("A Carton full of Champagne", 1967),
*Pohár od Pánaboha* ("A Cup from God",1971) and *Syn celerového
krále* ("The Celery King's Son", 1972), but the writer reached his

---

[1] Dukla, a football team.

best in two books of short stories, inspired by the nostalgia of his youth spent in the West-Bohemian countryside. While in *Smrt krás-ných srncù* ("Death of Beautiful Deer", 1971), the Holocaust overshadows Ota's early memories, in *Jak jsem poznal ryby* ("How I came to Know Fish", 1974), beautiful, sensitive descriptions of nature stand out. In both collections subtle human relationships exist; among the characters the somewhat quirky, lively father dominates the scene.

## How I Came to Know Fish

Fiction or childhood reminiscences? The two merge beautifully in Ota Pavel's book, where the single events are narrated in poetic language, full of nature imagery as well as of action and philosophical contemplation. Calm and patience, required for fishing, permeate the fifteen stories, each of which can be read separately despite the fact that Pavel's family history links them together and emerges clearly at the end. Ota and his two elder brothers have learnt the art of fishing from their father, an efficient travelling salesman whose great desire to own a fishpond is finally fulfilled, only to be marred by the Nazis who confiscate it. The defiant father and two elder sons are forced to go to three different concentration camps. Young Ota can stay with his gentile mother and later supports both of them by working in the coal mine. Poaching fish from the Wehrmacht helps relieve their starvation; it also provides considerable thrill for the reader when the boy takes greater risks than he imagines.

The first story, "Concert", recounts how Ota was initiated into angling. It sets the requisite quiet atmosphere for fishing, but gradually the narration brings tension and expectation, as in "The Death of Beautiful Deer", where the father risks his life by taking off his yellow star and going hunting for deer (strictly reserved for the Germans) in order to feed his two oldest sons. Although afraid of the Nazis and their collaborators, Ota, too, continues taking risks; the tension in "They Can even Kill you" reaches its peak when he is nearly caught, but an immense relief follows as the presumed collaborator proves to be the boy's rescuer. This kind of alternation makes Pavel's book eminently readable, especially for those with a strong sense of justice or who would like to escape from the hustle of daily life into the peaceful atmosphere of nature, where fish and other animals are treated with affection not only because they are beautiful but because they also provide life-saving food in crucial times. Although the wartime atmosphere and the constant fear for those in Nazi camps are deeply felt, the stories in *How I Came to Know Fish* radiate a strong family loyalty, peace and reconciliation.

In English

*How I Came to Know Fish,* Jindřiška Badal, Robert McDowell, trans., New York, New Directions, 1991.

# FERDINAND PEROUTKA

## *Budeme pokračovat*
("We Shall Continue")
Jiří Kovtun, ed., Toronto, Sixty-Eight Publishers, 1984

FERDINAND PEROUTKA (1895–1978), one of the greatest Czech journalists, was also one of Karel Čapek's closest friends and a public figure in the first democratic Czechoslovak Republic. He was born and bred in Prague (his father was inspector at the state railways) and entered the world of journalism soon after his grammar school studies.

He survived the six war years of his imprisonment in the concentration camps in Dachau and Buchenwald and returned to his chief-editorial position at the daily *Svobodné slovo* ("The Free Word", a sequel to *Lidové noviny* where the brothers Čapek used to work) and the weekly *Dnešek* ("Today"). In the years 1945–46 he represented the Cultural Freedom Party as their MP, but left his country after the communist *coup d'état* in 1948 for the exile in the UK and the US. There he soon became the leading spirit of Radio Free Europe.

His journalistic output is immense – the most important publication being his *Budování státu* ("Building of the State", 1933–36), concerning the history and politics of the first republic from 1918 onwards. But he was always keen on culture, not only in his essays. He also wrote fiction: his play about people's behaviour in various brink situations during the rise and fall of the Nazi Germany, *Oblak a valčík* ("A Cloud and a Waltz", 1948) came out as a novel, too. Inspired by history, he wrote a novel *Pozdější život Panny* ("Later Life of the Virgin", 1980) about Joan of Arc, whom Peroutka does not allow to suffer her death on the stake, but lets her live on to complete her heroic task.

## *Budeme pokračovat*

When F. R. Leavis described a work of literary criticism as journalistic, he meant it as a condemnation; he was practically denying journalists a place among writers. However, there are journalists with a difference, those who write prose and/or poetry as well and use the language of creative artists. Peroutka, the author of the collection of essays "We Shall Continue", certainly belonged to them, even if his contribution to pure fiction is comparatively small. This book contains a selection of Peroutka's broadcast speeches written between 1951 and 1977. For many Czechs who read or listened to them, Peroutka was a brilliant political thinker, but his essays on literature or culture in general are also numerous and no less excellent. All of them show his extensive general knowledge and formulate clearly his views on art and its place in life.

Chronologically arranged and carefully selected by Jiří Kovtun, Peroutka's essays reflect the political as well as cultural development in Czechoslovakia in the above-mentioned period, but one can start reading the book in the middle or end, if one is particularly interested in literature and pen portraits of writers like Karel Čapek, Karel Havlíček Borovský, Josef Škvorecký, Jan Drda, Julius Fučík, Karel Teige, Jarmila Glazarová, Dostoyevsky, Pasternak, Solzhenitsyn, or other contemporary public figures. Peroutka criticizes those who conformed to the prevailing political climate, but he gave them credit where credit was due, and writes impartially, even magnanimously, about those "whom one liked and didn't like". As a journalist and broadcaster in exile, he developed a powerful style that could hardly avoid occasional sweeping statements, but one can always admire the clarity of his thought and expression, the way he could hit the nail precisely on the head.

The writer and journalist Karel Havlíček Borovský (1821–1856) has a special place in Peroutka's heart and, consequently, in this book; the editor explains why: "As Havlíček is a good example of a 19th century liberal fate, F. Peroutka can be the same for the 20th century. Both experienced the bitterness of disappointment. For

Peroutka, there was more of both. He enjoyed twenty years of state independence and cultural flourishing, for which Havlíček could only long. He spent six years in a Nazi prison and thirty years in exile, from which he never returned." He had good reasons for pessimism but remained realistic, condemning the evil from which his country had to suffer in his lifetime.

The title "We Shall Continue" is significant. Peroutka used this phrase when he had more to say on the subject and the time allocated was not sufficient for him to develop the theme, so that he would continue in the next broadcast; here, symbolically, it indicates Peroutka's legacy to his nation to continue building its better future on good traditions, by the same liberal and fair means.

# JAN PROCHÁZKA

## *Přestřelka*
### ("A Skirmish")
Prague, Československý spisovatel, 1966

JAN PROCHÁZKA (1929–1971), was born to a farming family; after his studies at a school of agriculture he became manager of a state farm for young people. Like many idealists he favoured communism at first, but soon realized his mistake. He was sent to the frontier guards to do his national service there, but later took an active part in the liberation process in the sixties. However, in the tough years of the "normalization" after 1970, he became victim of a public campaign against him, which hastened his premature death. Even his funeral was supervised by the police.

Procházka contributed to a number of periodicals and established himself as a prolific script writer. His novel *Přestřelka* is his most extensive work, but he wrote many shorter pieces of prose, *Zelené obzory* ("Green Horizons", 1960); *Svatá noc* ("Holy Night", 1966); *Tři panny a Magdalena* (Three Virgins and Magdalena", 1966); *Kočár do Vídně* ("A Carriage to Vienna", 1967), to name a few. His *Ucho* ("The Ear"), which fittingly presents the dense atmosphere under the totalitarian government, was made into an attractive film in 1969, but it could not be shown until after the Velvet Revolution in 1989.

### *Přestřelka*

This substantial novel came out towards the end of the politically rather relaxing period before the Soviet invasion of Czechoslovakia;

after 1968 the new régime would have hardly liked to see a work published about the life of the frontier guards whose duty was to catch and, if need be, to kill, refugees fleeing from the communist Czechoslovakia to the free Austria. The eponymous skirmish refers to a clash in which frontier guards were wounded and one of the refugees committed suicide. But, against this background there is another – symbolic – "skirmish", namely a quarrel between the protagonist and his girlfriend whom he loves dearly. His employment duties prevent him from going promptly to see and pacify her, so that one part of the novel follows the life of Vojtěch, overshadowed by his constant fear lest she leaves him for good.

Apart from this line of action, the author develops another, more interesting, thread, namely events from the life of Vojtěch's girlfriend. In retrospect, we see scenes from the lives of the Czechs under the Nazi rule during the war, memories which remain as historical documents in this book of fiction. The comment on the blurb, stating that the novel reads like a thrilling detective story, may be true of Vojtěch's part, describing in detail various military operations; their extent, however, uninitiated readers may not greatly appreciate.

And the climax? The "skirmish" between the two young people is resolved happily, the lovers meet and are reconciled. The fact that in the real skirmish there are wounded people and a suicide, can be seen as a happy end only by communists serving the régime faithfully. As the author deals with the coarse military atmosphere, he feels obliged to use the appropriate jargon with its rough language, but – unlike some contemporary Czech writers who season their dull books with obscenities – Procházka would not offend sensitive readers. Passages in colloquial language read well and the ironic use of contemporary communist slogans adds a streak of humour as well as a special feeling of the political tension in the atmosphere.

The novel does not lack humanity: even in the dangerous military lives there is a place for kindness; for instance, when the protagonist is helping and supporting a family whose breadwinner is a political prisoner. The suicide and the wounded in the novel indicate a warning against the vanity and uselessness of such actions, but the soldiers see it rather as a natural part of their lives.

# LENKA PROCHÁZKOVÁ

## *Hlídač holubů*
### ("The Minder of Pigeons")
#### Köln, Index, 1987

LENKA PROCHÁZKOVÁ (born 1951), daughter of the writer Jan Procházka, suffered from political persecution: she was not allowed to finish her studies at the Faculty of Journalism at Prague, but could read and finish the course in theory of culture at the Faculty of Philosophy in 1975. She was unable to find a suitable post and had to do menial work. As a signatory of the Charter 77 she could publish only in *samizdat* and abroad. After the liberation in 1989 she became very active in public life, as a founder and/or committee member of several voluntary aid associations. Her main genre is prose, short stories and novels, but she also wrote scenarios and essays in journals, both in *samizdat* and in exile papers.

Her first novel, *Růžová dáma* ("The Pink Lady", Köln, Index, 1982), signals the main feature of her writings, the intimate relations between men and women where the latter often act as the stronger of the two; yet they seek in suitable partnerships refuge from the unpleasant and dangerous life, influenced by politics. The heroine of the novel *Oční kapky* ("Eye Drops", Toronto, Sixty-Eight Publishers, 1987) is a university-educated single mother whose selfish partner had escaped to exile in Germany; following him, she finally fails to administer the highly poisonous "eye drops", meant to kill them both. *Smolná kniha* ("The Book of Trouble", Toronto, Sixty-Eight Publishers, 1991) reflects the author's relationship with a dissident writer (presumably Ludvík Vaculík). Lenka Procházková also published collections of short stories, *Přijeď ochutnat* ("Come to Taste", Köln, Index, 1982), *Hlídač holubů* ("The Minder of Pigeons", Köln, Index, 1987), *Zvrhlé dny* ("Perverse Days", Prague, Primus, 1995), and a documentary/novelette *Pan ministr* ("The Minister", Prague, 1996) about the tragic fate of the Minister of Foreign Affairs Jan Masaryk. In *Šťastné úmrtí Petra Zacha* ("Lucky Demise of Peter Zach", Prague, Primus, 1997) she writes about some absurd situations during the Velvet Revolution. A grant in 1999 enabled her to stay for a year in the Bamberg International House of the Artists, where she wrote essays on various subjects, collected in *Dopisy z Bamberka* ("Letters from Bamberg", 2000); while there, she also compiled a short historical, somewhat controversial, novel about Christ, *Beránek* ("The Lamb", 2000).

## *Hlídač holubů*

The world of Procházková's stories is everyday life in a country where people are not free to travel abroad and feel as if they are in a cage ("Jenom splín", "Spleen"); where excitement is stirred by the rare availability of stew beef at the butcher's ("Domovník", "The Janitor") or by extramarital affairs which are supposed to brighten the dreariness of daily life ("Doutník na potom", "A Cigar for Afterward"); where the wives of political prisoners live in constant fear of house searches and suspect everyone of spying on them ("Host do domu", "A Guest in the House") and where gullible women are attacked and robbed as women are anywhere else ("A Cigar for Afterward"). The title story shows Procházková's gift for storytelling best: with gentle humour and irony she writes about a young man whose task is to chase away pigeons on the glass roof of the huge Palace of Peace so that they do not distract delegates of the communist party gatherings in the room below; the mixture of narration and interior monologue is very effective here, as it is also throughout the book, and generates a powerful tension as the hero, forgotten on the roof when the skylight is locked for the weekend at the meetings' conclusion, tries in vain to draw someone's attention to his plight.

The tragic title story stands out for its unusual subject as well, but the situations in most of the other pieces could be described as ordinary. Still, the subtleties of the characters' feelings and the liveliness of style throughout make Procházková's stories both interesting and readable.

# SYLVIE RICHTEROVÁ

## *Slabikář otcovského jazyka*
### ("A Primer of Paternal Language")
#### Atlantis/Arkýř, Brno/Prague, 1991

SYLVIE RICHTEROVÁ (born 1945), daughter of a plant pathologist and a grammar school teacher, studied language interpretation (French and Russian) in Prague (Ph.D. 1971) and Rome, but spent most of her working life in Italy, as a researcher, lectrice and professor of Czech language and literature. She taught at the Universities of Rome, Padua and Viterbo. Since 1974 she has been publishing articles and reviews about (mostly) Czech literature in learned periodicals, as well as poetry and prose. She has also translated Czech authors into Italian (Jan Skácel, Jiří Kolář, Věra Linhartová, Ludvík Vaculík) and contributed to radio and television.

Her creative writing is marked by ideas of the confusion and uncertainty in this world and a vain search for the purpose of human existence. This can be seen in her poetry (*Neviditelné jistoty,* "Invisible Certainties", 1994), but even more so in her three books of prose, listed and outlined below.

## *Slabikář otcovského jazyka*

It is just as well that Richterová's two earlier publications, *Návraty a jiné ztráty* ("Returns and other Losses", 1978), and *Místopis* ("Topography", 1983), are included in *Slabikář otcovského jazyka,* for all three are connected by their partly autobiographical conception. They also share the same, rather vain, search for some sense of human life, for one's identity, as well as the fear that these may never be found.

The heroine's (if she can be referred to as such in this very loose structure) childhood memories work as a stabilizing element in the life of a person who spends her early days under the communist rule and lives later in the free world as an exile. In their clarity, wit and terseness, these childhood memories are beautifully written – and so are the seemingly unconnected longer anecdotes which eventually complete the family picture as well as the background to it, the tribulations and humiliation to which the communist régime reduced its citizens. However, life abroad is uncertain, unsettling and full of fear; an individual is doomed forever to question its sense. Here the author communicates her feelings to the reader in short, philosophico-semantic paragraphs which at times disintegrate into very brief diary entries. As an experiment in form, these may well serve to indicate the turmoil in the speaker's mind, but do they really communicate with the reader successfully in this way? The author herself resents the lack of clarity in Sterne's *Tristram Shandy*,[1] but after the excellent beginning, when the excited reader rejoices in expectation of a good read, he or she may be disappointed by Richterová's extensive use of unconnected snippets, however meaningful they may be in themselves.

The author pays great attention to language. One must admire her use of puns, of phrases which radically change meaning in different contexts, even her unfinished sentences with their completions cleverly implied. She plays with the comma thoughtfully and exploits enumeration, paradox and double negatives to their fullest; even trivial actions from her daily routine sound interesting. Nevertheless, a language-conscious Czech reader may be disturbed by the frequent use of *ten stejný* instead of *tentýž*, just as a religious folklorist may resent that, instead of on Easter Monday, the – ancient or rather pagan – custom of chastising women is performed here on Easter Day.

Innovation, experimentation and the combination of fiction with philosophy may have their place in literature, but it seems a pity if they overshadow the purity and brightness of simple expression in the narrative, where Richterová's gift really lies.

---

[1] Lawrence Sterne (1713–68), *The Life and Opinions of Tristram Shandy, a Gentleman*, 1759–67.

# ZDENA SALIVAROVÁ

## *Honzlová*
Toronto, Sixty-Eight Publishers, 1972

## *Summer in Prague*
London, Harper and Row, 1972

ZDENA SALIVAROVÁ (born 1933) is a talented daughter of a publisher and bookseller. She studied dramaturgy in Prague, but also learnt singing and playing the violin. She became a member of two singing/dancing ensembles with whom she went on tour abroad, but this was later forbidden by the vindictive régime because her father and brother were accused of anti-communism. The harassment for the whole family was intensified after her father fled to the United States and her brother, later, to Canada. Salivarová married Josef Škvorecký in 1958, with whom she left for Canada in 1969.

Apart from the novel *Honzlová* she published short stories in periodicals as well as in a book form: *Panská jízda* ("Gentlemen's Ride", 1968), dealing with the varying male and female approach to love; and *Nebe, peklo, ráj* ("Heaven, Hell, Paradise", Toronto, 1976), which expresses – in a similar way as in *Honzová* – the contrast between honest people harassed by the régime and the conforming careerists who profit from their hypocrisy. Her last, epistolary, novel, *Hnůj země* ("The Muck of the Country", Toronto, 1994) records events from the lives of exiles who had left the communist Czechoslovakia in the first phase, the hard Stalinist era.

When the idea of establishing the Sixty-Eight Publishers came into being, practically from scratch, most of the burden rested on Salivarová's shoulders. She bravely carried out managerial, secretarial, editorial, technical and graphic work, as the need arose. Her reward of the Order of the White Lion and the honorary doctorate of the University of Toronto for that great achievement is fully deserved – the more so because she may have sacrificed to it a part of her talent and energy which, normally, she would have given to creative writing. Her literary work shows her lively, witty style, a fine sensitivity for presenting human relations and setting her characters into complicated situations.

## Honzlová

Salivarová has subtitled her best novel *Honzlová* a "Protest Song", for her heroine, Jana Honzlová, is trying hard to preserve her soul untainted by the pressures of the communist régime. It is a very sad book, but truthful and a real gem among other novels on the theme of survival in the totalitarian Czechoslovakia.

Like her husband, Josef Škvorecký, Salivarová, too, uses autobiography to advantage, particularly in the background to the novel. Her family, branded by the régime as "a class enemy", was forced to move into a small flat in a derelict block of houses in Prague, similar to the one where Jana Honzlová lives. She, too, is one of six children, although the fictional ones differ considerably from the real ones. Jana's father has fled into exile in the West, like Salivarová's, and, as the author herself mentions,[1] Jana's mother resembles her own most closely.

At twenty-one, Jana is the only breadwinner when, due to the distressing events in the family, her mother becomes apathetic; one brother is in prison for his attempt to leave the country into exile; another brother was sent to the penal regiment to do his national service; the eldest, rather selfish, sister, left the family when she found a job; the younger sister, flighty and irresponsible, is still too young to earn, as is the youngest, the ten-year-old Hugo. This good-

---

[1] *Samožerbuch,* Toronto, Sixty-Eight Publishers, chapter "Is *Honzlová* an autobiographical Novel?"

natured boy is Jana's best friend and support, in spite of his young age.

As a member of an artistic singing and dancing company Jana earns very little, so the family is nearly starving. They keep on refusing to conform or to become members of the communist party and, consequently, their fear of being persecuted increases their misery. But even the conformists with the régime seem nervous, uncertain and suspecting. Jana's colleagues' dislike of what they feel to be her moral superiority leads to their efforts to get rid of her from their midst.

At the opening of the novel Jana is alone in the company's office, copying music scores, while the rest of the ensemble is on tour in Finland; Jana, "unreliable", was refused a passport to go abroad with them, lest she would ask for asylum there. For all her feeling lonely and being rejected, she accepts her position stoically, as inevitable; in this state of mind she appreciates wholeheartedly the presence of an ally, the honest, hard-working cleaner of the office, Mrs. Pelikánová. She, too, believes in the good moral values of democracy, humanity and common sense and could be a firmer support to Jana than her mother, if she weren't doomed to die before the beneficial relationship of these two unlikely friends could mature. Salivarová describes with great compassion Mrs. Pelikánová's preparation for the Sunday lunch to which the hungry Jana was invited, but before the girl could enjoy the meal, she is shocked by her hostess's fatal heart attack.

As Jana was the only person present at the sad event, she is suspected of being possibly the cause of Mrs. Pelikánová's death – a pretext for the repressive apparatus to "rescue" her from the allegation, for the price of her becoming their informer. Cornered like this, Jana resists bravely, even more so when one of the ministry's officials repeatedly presses her, but eventually changes his tactics into courting her. Even in this dangerous position Jana continues to refuse this admirer (calling him "Bluebeard" in her mind) who is gradually becoming less official and more friendly. Yet, she cannot trust him and lives in constant fear of his potential reprisal. Her worry is aggravated by her mother's state of health, the older sister's meanness and the younger one's promiscuity. The only comfort now could be given by her earlier admirer, now a priest. She knows nothing about religion, has never been baptized, but sees now in baptism her best way to salvation. Her priestly friend grants this to her reluctantly because he understands her being motivated by despair rather than true faith.

The novel ends in tragedy. People who lived under the communist régime know only too well how difficult it was for the dwellers in state-owned blocks of flats to keep them in a reasonable state of repair, when the government didn't care to take necessary measures in time; in the novel, two courtyard galleries of Jana's home collapse, killing her beloved brother Hugo as well as one of the kind neighbours. The tragedy prompts "the Bluebeard" to act: he brings Jana a valid passport with a visa for France – a document which would have been coveted by many – but Jana, although at the end of her tether, refuses to be "rescued" in this way and decides to stay with her mother.

Jana's trials and tribulations illustrate very well the feelings of an individual, oppressed by the state, with its decay and spiritual poverty. Yet, Salivarová has a good sense of humour which she has embodied in her heroine. She used her as the main narrator, the whole novel thus flowing like a continual stream of consciousness which lends itself well to express directly Jana's thoughts, observations and feelings. Nasty, odious characters (like some members of the ensemble, or the autocratic cleaner succeeding Mrs. Pelikánová, or a few neighbours in the housing block) can be successfully treated in a novel with wit and gentle irony: there is still something of a slightly impudent child in Jana's nature to bring this about. She means well and expects other people to do likewise – until she realizes that the political poison has infected them too far; the apparatus is too strong for an honest individual to hold on with impunity to his/her own values.

Jana represents the idea that man is essentially good and that it is right to oppose evil; she acts with great courage, even when dangerous forces are against her. She sees her adversaries with some kind of regret that they don't know any better. And it is too late for her to appreciate that her firm stand has caused "the Bluebeard", a stiff party official at first, to change into a more human being. A charming streak is also brought into the novel by the cat Jůlinka and her five kittens, whom Jana "inherited" from Mrs. Pelikánová, and who take an active part in the family's life. Salivarová's witty, spontaneous style of writing makes them very much alive, but, as everything in the oppressive régime seems gloomy and unfriendly, poor Jůlinka soon becomes a victim of human cruelty, being killed by an unsympathetic neighbour. But all this is true to life, Jana's story being just one sample of an individual's life subjected to political pressures.

In English

*Ashes, Ashes, All Fall Down (Nebe, peklo, ráj),* Jan Drábek, trans., Toronto, Sixty-Eight Publishers, 1987.

*Summer in Prague (Honzlová),* Marie Winn, trans., London, Harvill Press, 1973.

# JOSEF ŠKVORECKÝ

## *Zbabělci*
("The Cowards")
Prague, Československý spisovatel, 1966

## *Příběh inženýra lidských duší*
("The Engineer of Human Souls")
Toronto, Sixty-Eight Publishers, 1977

JOSEF ŠKVORECKÝ was born in 1924 in Náchod (East Bohemia), to the family of a bank manager, an enthusiastic, active member of the patriotic gymnastics organization Sokol. Already during his grammar school studies Josef took delight in jazz, which copiously permeates his writings. As he finished these studies in the middle of the war (1943) when Czech universities were closed, he had to work – like most of his Czech contemporaries – as a labourer in munitions factories. Only after the end of the war could he start his university studies in Prague, one semester of medicine from which he switched over to English and philosophy. He spent his national service (1951–1953) with the tank corps – a source of inspiration for his subsequent satiric novel *Tankový prapor* ("The Tank Corps" 1971, translated by Paul Wilson as *The Republic of Whores*, Toronto, Knopf, 1993).

After a few years of grammar school teaching he worked as editor and contributor to prominent journals and in 1963 became a professional writer. But, already his novel *The Cowards* (1958) in which he too obviously glorified the western liberating army above the Russian, had antagonized the ruling communists; in 1969 he decided to leave with his wife, Zdena Salivarová, for Toronto where the University accepted him first as a Writer in Residence and later as a full member of staff, lecturing in Creative Writing and English, and American Literature. As a professor he stayed there until his retirement, but already in 1971 he had joined his wife in establishing the "Sixty-Eight Publishers" which enabled Czech exile writers (including themselves) as well as a host of blacklisted writers in communist Czechoslovakia to publish their works.

Škvorecký is a most versatile and prolific writer. Apart from many novels, novellas and short stories he produced numerous essays (on literature as well as general subjects), detective stories, film scripts, translations from English into Czech (Ernest Hemingway, William Faulkner, Sinclair Lewis, Raymond Chandler, Alan Sillitoe, William Styron). His best novels – like the two discussed below – are obviously autobiographical, but other works bear similar characteristics, too, e.g. *The Bassaxofone* (Prague, 1967), *Prima sezóna* (Toronto, 1975; "The Swell Season", London, 1982), *Povídky z rajského údolí* ("Edenvale Stories", Prague, 1995) – to name just a few. The novel *Lvíče* (Prague, 1969, translated as "Miss Silver's Past" by Peter Kussi, London, 1974) combines a love affair with a political, criminal story by way of a satire; politically motivated is also *Mirákl* ("The Miracle", Toronto, 1972).

Then there is a series of detective stories round the main character, the lieutenant Borůvka: *Smutek poručíka Borůvky* ("The Mournful Demeanour of Lieutenant Borůvka", Toronto, 1973), *Konec poručíka Borůvky* ("The End of Lieutenant Borůvka", Toronto, 1975), *Návrat poručíka Borůvky* ("The Return of Lieutenant Borůvka", Toronto, 1981) and "the detective divertimento" *Hříchy pro pátera* Knoxe ("Sins for Father Knox", Toronto, 1973).

In *Scherzo Capriccioso* (Toronto, 1984; "Dvořák in Love", New York, 1987, London, 1989) Škvorecký does not add any autobiographical aspects in his admiration of the great composer; he uses historical material while allowing his imagination to flow freely, yet without distorting facts. In *Nevěsta z Texasu* ("The Bride of Texas", Toronto, 1992), the American Civil War provides a colourful and tragic background for the escapades of a group of Czech emigrés, fleeing the oppression of the Habsburg Empire.

Among Škvorecký's novellas and short stories the following stand out: *The Bassaxofone, Babylonský příběh* ("The Babylonian Tale and other Stories", Prague, 1967), *Legenda Emöke* ("Emöke", London, 1978), *Sedmiramenný svícen* ("The Menorah", Prague, 1964;): the last, consisting of seven stories, shows the author's sympathy with the suffering of the Jews under the Nazis. In *Ze života lepší společnosti* ("From the Life of High Society", Prague, 1965) Škvorecký ridicules the unwarranted self-satisfaction of the Czech middle class, in an amusing mock heroic style used by a young schoolboy. *Konec nylonového věku* ("The End of the Nylon Age", Prague, 1967), dealing with a love triangle and reflecting the period of transition in the early years of the communist rule, when people still gave the régime the benefit of doubt, was written in 1950, but published seventeen years later, in the fairly liberal political atmosphere. In 1977 Škvorecký published his voluminous novel *Příběh inženýra lidských duší* ("The Engineer of Human Souls"), considered by many as his masterpiece.

In the literary world Škvorecký has a prominent place. He was awarded the prestigious Neustadt Prize by the University of Oklahoma in 1980 and, after the Velvet Revolution the Czechoslovak President granted him and his wife the Order of the White Lion. In 1992 the couple received honorary doctorates from the University of Toronto.

## The Cowards

*The Cowards* belongs to the class of fiction *débuts* in which the author's heart and mind overflow with feelings and ideas they wish to share with the reader. As Škvorecký's art as a novelist matured, he subsequently created a host of impressive works, but the appealing spontaneity and sincerity of *The Cowards* has not been surpassed by them.

The autobiographical aspect of the novel substantially contributes to the fluency of the writing. The hero, Danny Smiřický (who reappears in a few later novels by Škvorecký), was born in 1924, like the author, to a middle-class family in a small town in north-east Bohemia, where he, too, lives through the Second World War and experiences very dramatic historical events.

Actually, Danny is lucky; not only for his sheltered upbringing in the pre-war Czechoslovakia and most of the war years, but mainly because during the *Totaleinsatz* (total deployment) he could stay at home, while many of his contemporaries were forced to work in German factories; those born in 1924 were marked as "a special gift" to the Führer. Yet, bad enough, he had to work in a munitions factory (Messerschmidt) in his native town as soon as he had finished at his grammar school. As the Nazis had already closed all Czech universities in 1939 to punish and intimidate the "rebellious" Czech students, Danny could only dream about his future studies in Prague, as well as about "the girl he is to meet there". But the fact that the war was obviously nearing its end indicated that the dream was likely to become reality before long. The novel does not progress that far; all action takes place in one week, May 4–11, 1945.

Immature and inexperienced, Danny has a sensitive mind which is influenced by the uneventful provincial-town life; out of his numerous friends three are enthusiastic musicians – playing a trumpet, guitar and piano respectively. He joins them with his saxophone so to enjoy in jazz the happiest moments in his life. Through Danny's lively first-person narration it appears that he loves music even more than Irena, the girl he is very much longing for, but tries in vain to woo. As he wishes to impress her by daring, though not very sensible, behaviour, he gets into trouble with the occupying German authorities, only to be "rescued" by one of the town's worthies. A few days before the armistice, rather prematurely, Danny and his friends go round the town, obliterating German signs by black paint – but the Germans haven't fully surrendered yet and the real drama begins.

In the last stage of the war the local Czech patriots organize an anti-German resistance, expecting all able men to join. Danny and his friends do so rather reluctantly, as they are much more active and eager than the middle-aged, somewhat ineffectual organizers of "the revolution"; they are, in fact, the cowards, as they see them. Although Danny and his friends could be punished by their elders for disobedience if they took their own initiative, they do so – and succeed better than the organized group: the novel reaches its dramatic climax when Danny goes to fight the Germans effectively.

He joins his friend Přema (who had hidden a machine gun from the time of the 1938 mobilization) to actually destroy a German tank on its retreat from the advancing Russian army.

Like other young men, Danny, too, is concerned with girls and his efforts to find the best way to get through the dreary six war years. His love of jazz keeps his mental equilibrium when he measures up some ideas, "sacred" to the provincial society, and finds them wanting. He has no definite political views yet, although it is clear that he likes the English; a group of them pass through his town, together with masses of prisoners of many nationalities, liberated now from the Nazi concentration camps. As the Russian front is advancing, Danny ponders:

> Everything was tearing by so fast I felt lost in it all. I knew they'd (the Russians) be given a big welcome and that there'd be speechmaking and that everybody would be enthusiastic about communism and that I'd be loyal. I didn't have anything against communism, I didn't know anything about it for one thing, and I wasn't one of those people who are against something just because their parents and relations and friends are. I didn't have anything against anything, just as long as as I could play jazz on my saxophone, because that was something I loved to do and I couldn't be for anything that was against that. And as long as I could watch the girls, because that meant to be alive. (p. 392)

In spite of the tensions and horrors of the war described in the novel, or the boredom of the young people, the style of writing is fresh, many situations quite hilarious. The wit and humour here often originates in the language Škvorecký uses: it is colloquial, coloured by the north-east Bohemian dialect in which he was born and bred; rough expressions and four-letter words crop up abundantly, but – isn't it the way young men like to speak in order to appear more mature than they really are? Such people are the most prominent in this novel.

In this first important novel of Škvorecký he emerges as a born raconteur and an outstanding representative of the Czech post-Second World War prose.

### Příběh inženýra lidských duší

The theme of *The Cowards* continues and gets extensively

enlarged in this two-volume novel. Danny Smiřický appears here again, this time as a mature, though still single young man, a writer and university teacher of American and English literature at the fictional Canadian Edenvale College. The subtitle "An Entertainment on the old themes of Life, Women, Fate, Dreams, the Working Class, Secret Agents, Love and Death" clearly outlines the scope of this thickly populated work in which the author faithfully keeps his promise to the reader. As Robert Porter says, discussing *The Engineer of Human Souls,* "we are entering the workshop of a master craftsman" (*An Introduction to Twentieth Century Czech Fiction*, Sussex Academic Press, 2001, p. 104).

The author has divided the book into seven chapters, entitled by the names of masters of American and English literature, Poe, Hawthorne, Twain, Crane, Fitzgerald, Conrad, Lovecraft, respectively. This is relevant to Danny's teaching. Discussing their work with his students in the seminars, he who had experienced war, suffering under the Nazis as well as the communists, and had to live through the trauma of being an émigré, tries to interpret these works from a wider perspective of recent history than his sheltered, inexperienced ("innocent") students can grasp. Even a young, Harvard-educated lecturer seems to be taking inessential aspects (for instance, the symbolism of colour in *The Scarlet Letter*) in the study of the classics of literature, rather than explaining their philosophy of life and what can be derived from it for the present life. Danny/Škvorecký acts as an expert historian of literature.

Danny's students, free and open-minded, though limited by the strong influence of the fashionable cinema as well as their respective backgrounds, form, together with characters of various nationalities, only one part of Danny's world in the novel. The other – perhaps more important and emotionally involved – is his reminiscences of events in his young days in his native Kostelec; in fact, a narrative as if complementary to *The Cowards*. The same characters appear, but more are added, for instance, in the touching story of Danny's love relationship with the pretty Nadia, a poor factory worker, with whom he conspires to sabotage against the Nazis. Inexperienced as they are, they are soon found out, but the novelist twists the story so that they are spared the usual nasty consequences.

Hints about Nadia's terminal tuberculosis provide a lot of tension and true sadness when she eventually dies, shortly before the end of the war.

Nadia's story represents a romantic streak in the novel, but further events in the lives of Danny's Kostelec friends and acquaintances bring about sheer reality. The most remarkable case is, perhaps, the life of Přema, with his resistance to the Nazis and communist dominations, which produce some gory scenes in the novel; eventually he has to leave his homeland in order to find safety and freedom in Australia. Danny's nostalgia seems best revealed by his visit, years later, to one of his early girlfriends in Kostelec: he can hardly conceal his amazement when the door is answered by her daughter, almost an exact image of her mother when young.

All this contrasts sharply with the seemingly peaceful life of the diverse characters in the Canadian milieu. Not only do Danny's students (or their forefathers) belong to various nationalities, faiths and races, but Danny is even more concerned with his numerous compatriots living there, like himself, as refugees. They, too, are scarred by experiences similar to his, the memories of which still haunt them. However, now in safety, they lend themselves to be treated by a novelist with humour, as a caricature. But they have their problems, too: communist snoopers and informers try to penetrate the community; however, Škvorecký's contempt for them turns their actions into farcical brief detective stories.

Danny's associations of the past with the present link the two streams together in each chapter, but, interspersed, there are also numerous letters to Danny, which complete the amalgamating process of the novel. Most of them, too, are meant to amuse – by their writer's ridiculous spelling as well as their concern with their own, rather than Danny's, circumstances; yet, they supplement information, showing at the same time the mental distance between writer and addressee, the people who used to be close to another. Coincidence, fate, misfortune, all live hand-in-hand in this novel: Danny's friend from Kostelec, a Jewish girl named Rebecca, persecuted at home, takes refuge in Israel, only to see later her son and daughter-in-law being killed by a bomb there – when Danny remains as her only friend, far-away geographically as he may be. In the war-time Messerschmidt factory a very tense, dangerous atmosphere is created when the Czechs, very much against their will, have to sign their disapproval of the Reichsprotector Heidrich's assassination, but the modest Nadia acts as a *deus ex machina* when she pretends a fainting fit and falls into Danny's arms, so that both are thus removed from the abominable place at the crucial moment.

The scope of the novel is large in every respect, most of all in the number of the characters. The great narrator may have invented stories for each of them, but it would not be difficult for the reader to get lost among them, especially when a few of them have turned their coat (voluntarily or under pressure, like the priest who later becomes a member of the hateful communist state police), or when they appear somewhere else in the world of the novel. Škvorecký seriously exposes the cruelty of the two totalitarian régimes, as well as the nastiness of which man is capable; yet, the book abounds in his usual humour, the essence which helps people to get through difficult situations alive and well. He brightens his work with his wit and gentle irony, but he also enjoys writing openly about sex and sleaze, or indulging in a coarse, "masculine" type of humour. Perhaps one could recall the scene in a public lavatory where a Czech visitor to Canada should secretly hand over manuscripts of books written by authors blacklisted in Czechoslovakia, to be published in Canada. The place proves to be too public for the transaction, but, carried away by his imagination, the author, like a compulsive raconteur, describes the activities in the place in detail, spinning his scatological yarn ad absurdum – while half of it would have sufficed to amuse. But, perhaps one should also see the hidden meaning of such a scene, namely, Škvorecký's contempt for the communist régime and his joy in outwitting it: thanks to Sixty-Eight Publishers (founded and run by Škvorecký's wife Zdena Salivarová and himself), the blacklisted Czech writers weren't silenced. In this novel Salivarová appears as "my publisher Sandtnerová" and the book is dedicated to her.

Švorecký's wit and humour takes another form in the speech (or writing in the case of letters) of many characters, including the narrator himself. Not only that some use of the north-east Bohemian dialect, and Lojza's ignorant mixture of Czech and Slovak in his letters sound very funny, but English language influences the native speech of the Czech émigrés. They include in it mutilated English words or English idioms which either twist the meaning in Czech or make the sentence ludicrous. Characterized through their language, the Czech community in Canada looks grotesque – especially when represented by the unforgettable girl nicknamed Dotty. She dresses in a most eccentric way, her Czech vocabulary is nearly disappearing, while her language still preserves the Czech language structure. No doubt, Škvorecký enjoyed using his wit in this way, just as he was inventing absurd spelling mistakes in the letters written by people of varied intelligence and/or education. All this may be funny for Czech readers with a good command of English, but would those who have not got it, understand? The same question could be asked about the more serious matter, Danny's university-level interpretations of American and English novels: the Czechs may have heard about their authors, but how many (and here English-speaking readers should be included) would have actually read them to enjoy the novel fully? However, it is all functional – only, it seems that English-speaking readers using Paul Wilson's translation would benefit best.

In any case, the novel must be seen as a very dramatic picture of historical events during most of 20th century, of the people's mentality and their response to the world divided into East and West, with little mutual understanding. Its structure is loose – in fact, there is hardly any dominant climax. Loose ends remain loose, as life goes on: Danny has not married his Canadian youthful Irena, although he has had a chance and cared for her; the end of the novel dwindles in a trivial letter from Lojza, an epitome of a simple materialist conforming with the régime, as he knows not any better. At the time of the novel being written and published, no spark of political liberation had yet appeared on the horizon.

In English

*The Cowards*, Jeanne Němcová, trans., London, Victor Gollancz, 1958; Penguin 1972.

*The Mournful Demeanour of Lieutenant Borůvka*, Rosemary Kavan, George Theiner, trans., London, Gollancz, 1973.

*Miss Silver's Past (Lvíče)*, Peter Kussi, trans., London, Picador, 1974, Vintage, 1995.

*The Bass Saxophone; Emöke*, Káča Poláčková-Henley, trans., London, Chatto and Windus, 1978.

*The Swell Season (Prima sezóna),* Paul Wilson, trans., London, Chatto and Windus, 1983; Vintage, 1994.

*The Engineer of Human Souls,* Paul Wilson, trans., London, Pan/Picador, 1984.

*Dvořák in Love (Scherzo capriccioso),* Paul Wilson, trans., New York, Knopf, 1987; London, Hogarth Press, 1989.

*The Sins for Father Knox,* Káča Poláčková-Henley, trans., London, Faber and Faber, 1989.

*The End of Lieutenant Borůvka,* Paul Wilson, trans., Toronto, Lester and Orpen Dennys, 1989; London, Faber and Faber, 1990.

*The Return of Lieutenant Borůvka*, Paul Wilson, trans., London, Faber and Faber, 1990.

*The Miracle Game,* Paul Wilson, trans., London, Faber and Faber, 1991.

*The Republic of Whores* (*"Tankový prapor"*), Paul Wilson, trans., London, Faber and Faber, 1994.

*The Bride of Texas,* Káča Poláčková-Henley, trans., Toronto, New York, Knopf, 1996; London, Faber and Faber, 1996.

# JINDŘIŠKA SMETANOVÁ

## *Někdo přijde a nenechá mě zemřít*
("Someone Comes and Does Not Let Me Die")
Prague, Československý spisovatel, 1965

JINDŘIŠKA SMETANOVÁ (born 1923) finished her studies at the secondary school of economics in 1942 and held clerical posts, mainly in institutional libraries. She wrote a good number of essays and feuilletons for various periodicals, but was forbidden to publish after 1968. Consequently, she had to work only in inferior employment, but nevertheless continued to write scenarios and essays under borrowed names.

Smetanová is a gifted narrator who likes to give unusual, symbolic names to her works, and favours subjects from the everyday life of her characters. She published first a collection of short stories, *Koncert pod platanem* ("Concert under a Plane Tree", 1959), which was followed by a novelette *Růžové šaty ve vojenské torně* ("Pink Dress in a Soldier's Knapsack", 1963), dealing subtly with the strained relationship between parents and their children in two families, caused by a teenage pregnancy. Her full-size novel, *Někdo přijde a nenechá mě zemřít* ("Someone Comes and Does not Let me Die") came out in 1965. Life in the popular Neruda Street in Prague, which had already inspired writers in the past (Jan Neruda, Jakub Arbes, Vladimír Neff), stimulated Smetanová, too, in two collections of short stories, *Ustláno na růžích* ("The Bed Made of Roses", 1966) with its extended version *Ustláno na růžích a pod nebesy* ("A Four-poster Bed Made of Roses", 1970).

After the country's liberation Smetanová published another book of short stories, *Domovní důvěrnosti* (1990, "House

Intimacies") and she also prepared for publication an important document, the diary of her uncle JUDr. Antonín Schenk, President Masaryk's Private Secretary, 1928–37. It came out in 1996, entitled *T.G.M., "Proč se neřekne pravda?" (T.G.M.,* "Why Cannot Truth be Said?")

## *Někdo přijde a nenechá mě zemřít*

Smetanová's book "Someone comes and Does not let me Die" is her second in which she has chosen a long title for her novel, the first being "Pink Dress in a Soldier's Knapsack". What is the meaning of this? She deals here with life in a Czech border country village, previously inhabited by a German-speaking population, who has to leave for Germany after the war when the village is repopulated by Czech settlers. Looking back to the time of resettlement, one remembers that the number of pioneering enthusiasts was comparatively small, the "gold-digger" type being more frequent. People of various backgrounds thrown together rarely create a happy community; yet, by the late fifties, which is the time of Smetanová's story, the situation could have improved. In a way, it did; for in the despair of loneliness and frustration there is always someone who "comes and does not let you die": for the young, unbalanced, irresolute teacher, the friendship of a fourteen-year-old Slovak proves soothing; the same young boy rescues an old invalid lady singer by doing her shopping. Why has she come in her old age to this remote, isolated little place except to die? A postmaster, a communal farm manager and a few families live here without knowing exactly why they have come; they have been settled rather than settling themselves. Their occasional flashes of initiative are marred by orders of communist authorities, and experience teaches them that it will not pay to disregard them, however nonsensical they may be. The result is general passivity:

> When Karol Chudík deposited the cement bags into the passage in the farm and one of them slipped down, people skirted it, stepped over it, but did not lift it. Hološ looked in amazement to see how they were tripping over the bag, walking round it but not taking any notice of it as long as he didn't say, "Go lift the bag and put it on top; can't you see that it had slipped?".

A sociologist might be particularly interested in this gloomy picture of a set of rather aimless individuals as Smetanová has drawn them. She does not try to solve the problem of resettlement, which obviously still remains a bit of a problem after all the years; she is mainly concerned with the mental state of her characters who develop in the course of the novel, in spite of the deliberately loose links of their relationships. Smetanová has a fine touch when analysing the feelings of single individuals who attract each other at one time and repel at another; but closer human ties, a real community, cannot develop even if there *is* somebody "who comes and does not let you die".

# JAROSLAV STRNAD

## *Zrcadlení*
("Reflections")
Prague, Ivo Železný, 1994

## *Cesta do Damašku*
("The Road to Damascus")
Prague, Primus, 1994

JAROSLAV STRNAD'S (1919–2000) study of law in Prague was interrupted by the Nazis' closure of all Czech universities in 1939, so that
he could finish it only after the war. During the Nazi occupation of
his homeland he was imprisoned for three years in the concentration camp in Dachau and was persecuted later by the communists,
too. He had to change his employment frequently and was also
imprisoned for six months. In fact, he couldn't practise as a lawyer
(except in his novel "The Road to Damascus"), not even after his
escape to West Germany in 1950. In 1951 he was granted asylum in
Switzerland and built up a very productive career in Radio Free
Europe and as an editor and contributor to exile periodicals. His
earlier experience provided him with enough material to create in
his works a world of adversity, horror and evil, in which his heroes
struggle to preserve their lives, integrity and self-esteem. Strnad
developed a powerful expression: his vivid descriptions can often be
measured up with Conrad's (e.g. the hanging body of Mr. Hirsch in
*Nostromo*), but his wit and sense of humour provide a comic relief
in tense situations, too.

His first novel, *Job* (Zurich, 1976), depicts the suffering hero's tribulations in a D.P. (Displaced Persons') camp; *Prohry* ("Failures", "Losses", London, Rozmluvy, 1982) opens a large canvas of victims of the war, a variety of human nature acting under pressure and threat: as soon as the poor sufferer gets hold of a stick, he exercises his power in the same way as his oppressor did. After *Cesta do Damašku* and *Zrcadlení*, which also tend to examine the darker side of human nature and experience, Strnad wrote his memoir, the *Panoptikum* (1999). His own life was so full of unusual events that only a fraction could be incorporated into his novels: if his tragic heroes appear shrouded in emotion and pity to provide drama, the *Panoptikum* is no fiction, but sheer reality. The author looks back with his characteristic wit, seeing also the comic side of the horrors he had to face.

## *Zrcadlení*

In this psychological novel Strnad has attempted a deep analysis of a human soul fallen victim to the dark forces trying to break unsuspecting independent minds. His hero, the Czech refugee K.S., lives in Switzerland and seems to be adapting well to the security of a small provincial society under the wing of his caring, sensible Swiss wife. In this capitalist, apolitical society he has to maintain secrecy concerning his past and his assumed name because his new co-citizens would not understand – and he knows only too well that communist vengeance can strike opponents even in the safest country. He cherishes the idea of owning his dream house which he will build when he wins half a million in the lottery; but the memory of his dreadful experiences before his escape prey upon his mind, and insignificant events rekindle his fears and feed his growing persecution mania. A chance meeting with his great early love after many years upsets his emotional balance and leads to tragedy, as K.S., in a paranoid fit, shoots his former lover as well as himself only moments before the news about the lottery win reaches him.

The powerful effect of K.S.'s gradual mental and emotional disintegration is achieved by a masterly handling of numerous flashbacks, reflecting K.S.'s past life, particularly his unfortunate relationship with his father, a high police official. There are also glimpses into the purges of students, the torture of political prisoners, frontier incidents, and links with western intelligence services. All this is skilfully packed into a modest-size yet powerful novel which, in spite of its tragic theme, includes goodly portions of Strnad's usual caustic humour: K.S.'s dreams about his past may horrify, but visions of his dream house amuse; allergic fits of sneezing evoked by sexual excitement create comic situations – and save the author from the potential need of describing dramatic bedroom scenes. Strnad's witty language also relieves the effects of the tensions and emotional turmoil in the hero's mind; it is firm, virile and never crude.

## Cesta do Damašku

Symbolically, this book is a novel of conversion, not of the central character whose Christian humility and faith are firm enough, but of Judge Toman who enters the scene later than the devotee Jan Krása but dominates it up to the dramatic end. Actually, he undergoes a double conversion: a sincere communist and atheist at first, he gradually sees the corruption and moral decay of the régime; and, driven into a narrow corner, he also turns to God for help.

Himself a lawyer, Strnad skilfully exposes the abuse of law which could easily succeed in destroying the consciencious objector Krása, a Christ-like figure of absolutely uncompromising moral and religious principles, ready to suffer for them rather than betray them; but truth prevails in the end and Krása is saved. He suffered for his views earlier in the Nazi camp, where he miraculously escaped death; he practically saved Toman's life there and did a good turn as well for another mate, who later tries to return the kindness by helping Krása in his effort to extricate himself from his unfortunate involvement with the communist law. Krása's almost superhuman faith in Christian principles gives the necessary tension to the novel and eventually also presents a difficult dilemma to Toman, now Krása's judge at the trial: defending the most natural human rights, Krása has inadvertently caused the death of a communist policeman. His remorse and his insistent plea of guilt makes his defence almost impossible and leads to the most powerful part of the novel, the judge's increasing disillusionment with communism and his masterly rescue of both Krása and himself.

While the horrors of Nazi camps continue to linger in human memory, life under communism seems to be fading in people's minds. Strnad's novels should be read, for they show the human soul exposed to all the invisible crippling effects which only the strongest can resist. Sooner or later, such forces were capable of cornering anyone; the non-interfering Krása survives only by a miracle, but Toman's humanity struggles with evil forces which mark him forever.

# MARIE ŠULCOVÁ

## *Brána věčnosti*
("The Gate of Eternity")
Prague, Melantrich, 1997

## *Prodloužený čas Josefa Čapka*
("Extended Time of Josef Čapek")
Prague, Paseka, 2000

MARIE ŠULCOVÁ was born in 1926, a daughter of a police officer. After her grammar school studies she worked as a clerk until her family duties occupied her fully. She has always been interested in history and wrote well from her childhood. In the thirties her father was appointed Chief police officer in Chýše, West Bohemia, where the family spent about ten years. The local castle, belonging to Count Lažanský, was the place where Karel Čapek spent five months in 1917 as a tutor to the Count's son; the fact led Šulcová to study the writer's life and work, to become eventually his and his brother Josef's most prolific biographer.

With her talent for writing fiction she chose the form of *biographie romancée* for her series of books about the brothers Čapek, but her interest in history combined with her love of truth and honesty ensures the credibility of important details in her writings. The fact that she could actually talk to people who knew her "characters" personally provides further assurances about the authenticity of her statements. The first two out of the six volumes on the Čapeks came out under the communist régime, when writing about such liberal authors was possible only with great caution; after the liberation, one can sense Šulcová's relish in referring freely to Karel's famous anticommunist essay (1924) or exposing the destructive efforts of the communists, as the post-war free Republic (1945–1948) was trying to establish itself among the free European states.

These are the titles of her sequel on the Čapeks: *Kruh mého času* ("The Circle of my Time", Plzeň, Západočeské nakladatelství, 1975); *Čapci* ("The Čapeks", Prague, Melantrich, 1985); *Ladění na dvě struny* ("Tuning for Two Strings", Prague, Melantrich, 1990); *Poločas nadějí* ("Semifinal of Hopes", Prague, Melantrich, 1993); *Brána věčnosti* ("The Gate of Eternity", Prague, Melantrich, 1997); *Prodloužený čas Josefa Čapka* ("Extended Time of Josef Čapek", Prague, Paseka, 2000).

Apart from these works, she wrote fairy tales, a novelette *Šance pro Ondřeje* ("A Chance for Andrew", 2006), about a family with a seriously sick child, and a historical study about Antonín Marek, a liberal and patriotic priest (1785–1877), entitled *Libuňský jemnos-tpán* ("The Gentleman of Libuň").

## Brána věčnosti

Like all of Šulcová's books on the Čapeks, this one, too, qualifies as a fictional biography, but, necessarily, the documentary element now prevails. It is evident how painstaking she was in preparing her extensive background material, how she was more concerned with fact than fiction; although exact references are not given, the details mentioned can be readily verified in the listed sources. Having lived through these historical times herself, Šulcová possesses a personal involvement that makes her writing significantly poignant, as it should be in a novel: the reader can feel her sharing Karel Čapek's fears for the country under the slogans of Hitler's propaganda and the disturbances of the incited Sudeten Germans in the late thirties, or her sorrow over the fate of the Czech populace driven from their border-country homes after Munich, or over the dejected Czech army returning at the same time from their posts for demobilization. Yet, judging these events from the perspective of half a century, Šulcová sounds more factual than sentimental; she even embarks bravely on intricate political debates, as Karel Čapek himself used to do with his brother and friends.

The prevailing factual element in the book offers very interesting reading and should be praised, even if it occasionally pushes the protagonist off the main stage; the size of the work allows him to grow fully as a character, nevertheless. At this time Karel Čapek was reaching the peak of his creative activity and becoming the most prominent spokesman on behalf of progress, truth, freedom and honesty; but Šulcová also had to deal with the delicate subject of his belated marriage to Olga Scheinpflugová, which resulted in a cooling off of his close relations with his family. Combining fact with poetical licence, Šulcová the novelist has created very credible characters in Karel Čapek himself and, perhaps even more true to life, in Olga, not to mention their relatives and friends who played significant parts in their lives.

For all the wealth of information, the book *does* read as a novel, a novel about a great writer but also about a nation struggling for the preservation of its freedom and identity in spite of adversity. "The Gate of Eternity" was meant for those who "tend to forget as well as those who know next to nothing about this chapter of our (Czechoslovak) national history, so that it is mere legend to them".

## Prodloužený čas Josefa Čapka

The author has called the fifth and closing volume of biographical novels on the brothers Čapek "The Extended Time of Josef Čapek". Perhaps we should interpret the word *extended* in relation to Josef's younger brother Karel, who died prematurely less than three months before Hitler occupied their homeland, while Josef, imprisoned by the Nazis from 1 September 1939, spent his "extended" years in concentration camps at Dachau, Buchenwald, Sachsenhausen, Berlin and Bergen-Belsen. He died in the last-named one a few days before the camp's liberation in April 1945, the exact date unknown.

Šulcová knew enough from hearsay and study about the horrors of these camps to be able to reconstruct vividly Josef's life and martyrdom there; in addition, her poetic creativity led her to imagine Josef's thoughts as a prisoner, his hopes for the future as well as his memories of his past, happier life. The combination of present and retrospective views adds poignancy and tension to this

novel with a tragic hero. Yet, the background to the novel is on a much larger scale than just Josef's life in the camps. The author refers to the book as a "factographical novel", distancing herself from appearing as a historian, but a true historian would not find much fault in her detailed, fact-based descriptions of the period. She lived through this period and also met a number of people who knew the Čapeks personally.

In fact, this last volume of the series pays homage not only to the brothers Čapek, but also to the thousands of unknown heroes who perished through the war. Šulcová graphically reconstructs how Czech people of all classes and positions lived and behaved then, bravely recording events which should be remembered by posterity and the lessons which should be learned from them. The effort of forty years which the author spent on her work on the brothers Karel and Josef Čapek deserves to be crowned with laurels.

# MILOSLAV ŠVANDRLÍK

## *Černi baroni*
### ("The Black Barons")
Prague, Mladá fronta, 1991, 3rd edition

MILOSLAV ŠVANDRLÍK was born in 1932. Both of his parents enjoyed amateur acting; before Miloslav started his study of acting and play-producing at the Academy of Drama in Prague (1951), he learnt about the subject at the City Music School. He worked as a labourer for nearly a year and completed a course for labourers to qualify for university. After two years, however, he had to leave. He became a successful script writer, working for the radio and television.

Švandrlík has made a name for himself as a humorist and satirist, having published numerous short prose pieces and scenarios which show his great gift for inventing and describing comic situations. This is true also about his more substantial works in which he mostly concentrates on the development of one comic strain – rather than delving into the inner world of his characters. The novel *Černí baroni* ("The Black Barons") is undoubtedly his most successful work, but out of his other humorous writings at least a few should be mentioned: *Pražská strašidla* ("Prague Ghosts", 1968), *Draculův švagr* ("Dracula's Brother-in-law", 1970), *Dívka na vdávání* ("The Girl Ready to be Married", 1983), *Starosti korunovaných hlav* ("Worries of the Crowned Heads", 1986), *Šance jako hrom* ("A Terrific Chance", 1989). His political satires could not be published during the communist régime: "The Black Barons" first came out in Zurich in 1969, under the pen-name Rudolf Kefalín.

After the Velvet Revolution Švandrlík developed further the theme of "The Black Barons" in *Říkali mu Terazky* ("They Called him Terazky", 1991) and wrote a great many shorter humorous pieces.

## Černí baroni

Can one really blame a victim of torture for taking revenge when eventually the opportunity to do so with impunity offers itself? The Velvet Revolution in Czechoslovakia in 1989 brought a great relief; people could speak freely again and, consequently, some very rough material emerged in this particular book. Perhaps there should have been warnings such as: very strong, foul language, rough, brutal scenes, violence, inhumanity, physical and moral filth? For men only?

Yet, Švandrlík's "The Black Barons" isn't lacking in literary merit. It scored highly on the book market of the early nineties, as most Czechoslovak young men suffered in one way or another during the compulsory national service, especially during the hard Stalinist era, under the despicable Minister of Defence, Alexej Čepička. The target of Švandrlík's satire is a special class of labour units (where the author himself had to serve), formed for the "re-education of the enemies of socialism"; mainly those who were disinclined to sing the marxist tune, like religious leaders, Jehovah's Witnesses, kulacks, the intelligentsia, but also disabled people, apart from burglars, criminals, violent offenders and, above all, alcoholics who lead in numbers in this book. As they are badly treated, their natural defence is cheating and cruelty – in order to survive. Even the normal national service under the communists was unpopular and notorious for being run by ignorant, uneducated marxists, building their careers on conformity rather than intelligence and expertise. "The black barons" were getting the worst.

No doubt that a lot of what happens to them in the book is true; but the author has also used his vivid imagination and poetical licence liberally. He is a gifted narrator, spinning the comic yarn *ad absurdum* – sometimes with an obvious effort; the tension then has to be broken somehow – at times, surprisingly, this happens by an unexpected calm induced by an officer's sheer ineffectuality to find a commensurate punishment for the offending soldier who expected the worst.

As a novel, the work is a thickly populated mosaic of events, connected very loosely by a character called Kefalín, an actor by profession, who, like the rest, muddles through, counting impatiently the days when, at last, he could be released. Only a few other characters can be distinguished in the novel (though there are quite a few names), but two officers are likely to impress themselves into the reader's memory: they are characterized by their speech mannerisms, one frequently using the expression "terazky" (a slightly mutilated Slovak word meaning "now"), the other indulging in a funny use of rhetoric questions, such as: "Now, I'll introduce to you the new leader of the group, comrade lieutenant Pavol Mazurek, to whom I'm handing over what? To whom I'm handing over the word to talk to you" (p. 205). When this mannerism is used in an emotional state – excitement, upset, anger – the comic effect is guaranteed.

The author's wit and an unusual sense for turning any situation into comedy, combined with his own experiences, led to the creation of his hilarious, rougher than Švejkian, farce where the comic strain springs from the officers' stupidity, the army's futile bureaucracy and political jargon; but in the background there is always lurking the nation's tragedy of both material and spiritual waste and damage: the beautiful old church in Zelená hora , one of the national treasures, is used by the unit as a storehouse; useful experts have to waste their talent for two years working as woodcutters, plaster/mortar mixers or tending pigs – the last actually providing the happiest times for poor Kefalín in his detestable national service. For all the author's wit, the survival of the fittest is blood-stained in this book.

# JAN TREFULKA

## O bláznech jen dobré
### ("Praise only for the Fools")
Prague, Petlice, 1973; Toronto, Sixty-Eight Publishers, 1978

JAN TREFULKA was born in 1929 in Brno and went to school with Milan Kundera, his good friend. In 1950 he was expelled from the communist party as well as from his study of literature and aesthetics at the Charles University in Prague. When he later resumed it at Brno, he could not finish it either. He had to earn his living with menial work, but between 1955 and 1970 he worked as an editor for journals and publishers. When his country regained its freedom in 1989, he became president of the Association of Moravian Writers.

Already in 1949 he criticized the politically conforming poetry and he published in 1962 his first, autobiographical novel, *Pršelo jim štěstí* ("Good Luck was Showered on them"), about his clash with the communist authorities; Milan Kundera used a similar subject later in his novel *The Joke* (1967). The following three collections of short stories, *Tři-sta-třiatřicet stříbrných křepelek* ("Three Hundred and Thirty-three Silvery Quails", 1964), *Výmysly* ("Fictional", 1966) and *Nálezy pana Minuse* ("Mr. Minus' Verdicts", 1966) signal Trefulka's interest in the daily lives of ordinary people. His novel-ette *O bláznech jen dobré* ("Praise only for the Fools", 1973) and the prose piece *Svedený a opuštěný* ("Seduced and Betrayed", 1983) could be published only in *samizdat* and abroad, respectively. In *Velká stavba* ("A Great Progress", 1973) Trefulka depicts absurdities of the ways in which a "socialist" society is formed; in *Zločin pozdvižení* ("The Criminal Uprising", 1978) he records the history of the workers' non-political strike in 1920. The four short stories, collectively entitled *Vraždy bez rukavic* ("Murders without Gloves", 1992), published after the fall of communism, deal freely with the traumatic 20-year period of the Soviet occupation of his country. In 1998 Trefulka's works published in *samizdat* were reprinted as a collection called *Bláznova čítanka* ("A Fool's Reader").

## O bláznech jen dobré

From the beginning of his career as a prose writer Trefulka has been interested in the psychology of characters muddling through the grey dullness of ordinary life. For those who were not directly persecuted by the communist régime, life was dull enough, but in the sixties when Trefulka started to write, a spark of hope for something better appeared on the political horizon. Although Trefulka's attitude towards conformity with the régime seems somewhat ambivalent at first, ranging from his membership in the party to being expelled from it, the fact remains that, after the Soviet invasion of his country, he could publish only abroad or in the *samizdat*.

His slim contemporary novel "Praise only for the Fools" is concerned with the search for a true identity and dignity of the protagonist, Cyril Duša, "the fool", now sixty-three-years old. He has always been a conformist, willing to do anything that was normally expected of him in the various stages of his earlier life: he was a manual worker at first, then a farmer; he joined the communist party and accepted his inferior place when his farm became communal. Later he was promoted to be director of a tractor station – but even that was rather unexciting; only his small private vineyard (allowed by the state in the days of collectivization) gave him some pleasure. He got married, as everybody else did; he had not much love for his unattractive and bossy wife, but he had very little choice and did not even make an effort to do better. "He wouldn't have protested if he had been asked to give up drinking wine because his Duša body and soul belonged to the state and he would never attempt deliberately to harm it" (pp. 21–2). Why has he always been so soft, so compliant, he wonders.

With such thoughts about his life in retrospect we meet him at the beginning of the novel, as he is leaving hospital after an operation. He is convinced that the doctors have discharged him only because they could not do anything more for him: surely, they didn't wish to tell him that he had terminal cancer? As if alienated from his previous life, he decides to enjoy the remaining part of his life to the full. In the eyes of the community he behaves like a fool when he leaves his wife as well as his dear vineyard and moves to a derelict building to live with Eva, a woman forty years his junior. She may be a dubious character, but life had treated her badly so that she didn't know any better; she is attractive, grateful, fully appreciating Duša's devotion to her: at last, a person whom she can trust! Eva goes to work and Duša, a pensioner, proves to be a very good housekeeper and cook, but, alas, their idyll cannot last, as society interferes. His wife applies for a divorce, his son appeals to him to be more sensible.

The son's voice, rather than the wife's, causes turmoil in Duša's mind. The first signs of his faltering upsets Eva who disentangles the situation: at a convenient moment she disappears with Duša's savings without trace. Was he really a fool to sacrifice everything for a few moments of human freedom and happiness? Going back to his wife would mean his defeat: instead, he can use his talents in the local tourist trade by becoming a manager and guide in a nearby cave. Living on his own quite a distance from the community means a gradual cure from his emotional shock, but as he grows older (and is far from suffering from cancer), solitude becomes difficult to bear and brings him back to his wife and the dear vineyard. Yet, it is not the return of a penitent, but of a person who got away from common conventions and found his self-respect in enjoying a taste of personal freedom.

In this very readable prose Trefulka uses the method of the protagonist's self-analysis, looking for reasons which make life dreary. Duša finds fault within himself, in his unselfish tendency to please others even in cases which seemed to him doubtful; yet, acting freely as he did later, makes him realize that there is a price to pay for true liberty.

Trefulka concentrates here fully on drawing the protagonist. Compared with him, the other characters are mere sketches, though clear enough for the parts they play. Through them, with Duša's reflections on life, as well as through his diary, Trefulka has created a truly interesting "fool". The diary, written in a rather primitive style and erratic spelling and punctuation, indicates a person of only limited education – yet, such people, too, have the right to be free and live in harmony with their own personality.

While many Czech contemporary writers are deeply concerned in their works with the political background, in Trefulka's novel this aspect is less important. Unobtrusive references to certain events date the work, but the stress is on the hero's sense of personal freedom, even if he appears a fool.

# LUDVÍK VACULÍK

## *Sekyra*
### ("The Axe")
Brno, Atlantis, 1966; 4th edition, 2003

LUDVÍK VACULÍK was born in 1926 in Brumov, Moravia, and spoke first the distinct local dialect. He received his middle-school education at the Baťa works in Zlín and, from 1946, he studied at the School of Politic and Social Sciences of Prague University where he graduated in 1950. He became editor of the communist daily *Rudé právo*, worked for the radio and, from 1965, in the editorial office of *Literární noviny*. His authorship of the "2000 words" manifesto (1968) clearly indicates his farewell to communism – which meant that his writings could not be officially published. In 1973 he instigated the secret edition Petlice where he edited about 400 works by blacklisted authors, including himself. Although subjected to political persecution and frequent interrogation, he signed the Charter 77.

He wrote and edited numerous essays, published in Petlice or other *samizdat* establishments or abroad, e.g. *Jaro je tady* ("The Spring is Here", Köln, Index, 1988), *Chvála bláznovství* ("In Praise of Folly", 1979), *O čem bych psal, kdybych měl kam* ("What I Would Write about if I Knew Where to Publish" , 1974), *Hodina naděje* ("An Hour of Hope, Czech Literature 1968–1978"); among his more substantial works, *Rušný dům* ("A Busy House", 1963) about the life in a hostel for young working people, and *Sekyra* ("The Axe", 1966) were published officially.

His experimental, Orwellian novel *Morčata* came out in Petlice , 1973, and in Toronto, Sixty-Eight Publishers, 1977 ("The Guinea Pigs", New York, Penguin Books, Inc., 1973); *Český snář* ("A Czech Dream Book") only in Toronto, Sixty-Eight Publishers,

1983. Apart from dreams, this last-named, voluminous book, also registers diary entries, memories and documentary autobiographical events, tinged with fiction; it can be described as a picture of Czech society in the seventies, as seen by a dissident. In another diary-type book, *Milí spolužáci!* (1939–45, "Dear Schoolmates!"), published in Köln, Index, 1986, the documentary and epistolary prevails. After the Velvet Revolution Vaculík published a novel concerning unfaithfulness and jealousy as it occurred in his own life, called *Jak se dělá chlapec* ("How a Boy is Made", 1993), and in 2002 its free sequel *Loučení k panně* ("Farewell to the Virgin").

## Sekyra

Like many Czech writers in the middle of the last century, Vaculík, too, believed that communism was the right reaction to the hated Nazism. But soon these writers felt betrayed when they found the rigidity of the régime, scheming and abusing the idealism of their adherents. They tried, particularly during the promising Dubček era, to influence the ideology to become more human. In 1966, when *The Axe*, Vaculík's early novel on the subject, was published, nobody could foresee how cruelly the people's hopes would be dashed two years later by the Soviet invasion.

The work could be described as a generation novel, with many autobiographical characteristics, the hero and narrator, a Prague journalist, being the most important. The action moves in three time levels – the past, present and future: while the very first, brief sentence states that the protagonist was just going to pay his first visit to his "brother-the bus driver", already in the second time level the scene is their native home, his brother just born, the narrator ten years old. They were born to the poor family of a village joiner in the thirties of the last century, the family being so poor that the father went to Persia for several years to earn enough for them. Yet, their life in the picturesque East-Moravian village surrounded by beautiful nature looks idyllic. The childhood values are the most constant, stable element in the changing world. The family members keep on returning to the place which provides new strength in the chaos in which they find themselves after having left it in search of livelihood.

This is true mainly about the father and son, the two main characters. But just as Vaculík's narration moves on three time levels, the episodes or important events happen in several locations, be it the visit at "the brother-the bus driver's", or the narrator's Prague editorial office (where his conflicting ideas about communism originate), or the father's engagement on a large communal farm where he moved after his wife's death. His diary entries from this period (showing the true picture of the dishonesty and mismanagement of the bureaucratic leaders of state farms), as well as his letters from Persia earlier on, complement the material of the novel most effectively.

At first, the young son sees the role model in his self-educated father, an idealist communist, but he leaves the home to be educated and finds himself alienated from his father and his own profession, influenced by the ideology in which he soon ceases to believe. The son's conflict with the father is intensified when the latter becomes – as a privileged, loyal communist – manager of a large state communal farm. He is determined to do well to please the authorities, but his position allows him a closer look into the inefficiency and corruption of the party-governed society. He, too, begins to have his doubts; especially in the company of his son he feels uncertain, wavering. Both father and son feel the loss of old values when they see the rural society changing with the passing of time and the new way of life. Vaculík deals with the father/son relationship with a remarkable subtlety, in his concise style of writing where an implication often extends considerably the meaning of a brief remark.

Strangely enough, the main characters have no names: the father is just "dad", the other members of the family are referred to as "my brother, the bus driver", "my brother who is in Slovakia", "the Prague son", "the wife of my son", "the cousins of Tarandová"; this method helps to indicate that, in certain episodes, his brothers act as grown-ups, or that his son is married, etc. The whole novel is a collection of episodes or stories, the end of each suggesting a reason to unfold the next, be it at a different time or place. In this way the narration flows smoothly and spontaneously. The episodes permeate each other like an endless stream-of-consciousness, the characters being alive and distinguished by their colourful speech.

As Vaculík was born in East Moravia where a distinctive dialect is spoken, he uses it in places – somewhat incorrectly and inconsistently (for the Czech readers to understand?). Not withstanding, the dialect plays an important part in the novel, as it indicates the original way the peasants think, the peculiarity sounding rather funny. But Vaculík can make even a serious situation comic; for instance, early in the novel, when the poor family can at last buy enough material to build their own dwelling. When the beams for the roof are stolen from them, the horrible fact causes a moral twist in the suffering party's mind. Surprisingly, the roof is being erected quite soon thereafter, but the male members of the family, the builders themselves, refuse to explain where the new beams come from. "Don't ask and you won't be blamed", they say, while another curious member, grasping the meaning, comments: "Oh, God, the world today is full of thieves!" Vaculík has an excellent sense of humour, the source of which can be traced in his homeland dialect.

*The Axe* is an important novel – one of the first bravely announcing the people's longing after freedom from the communist yoke.

In English

*The Axe,* Marion Sling, trans., London, André Deutsch, 1973.
*The Guinea Pigs.* Káča Poláčková, trans. London Magazin Editions, 1974; New York, Penguin Books, Inc., 1975.

# MICHAL VIEWEGH

## *Účastníci zájezdu*
### ("Participants of a Holiday Trip")
### Brno, Petrov, 1996

MICHAL VIEWEGH (born 1962), studied Czech and Education at Prague University, having compiled his diploma essay on the subject of a teacher's role in relation to the Czech and world fiction. After a brief teaching career he became a publisher's reader and also a professional writer. He first published short stories in prominent periodicals, as well a prose piece with a detective plot, *Názory na vraždu* ("Opinions on Murder", 1990). In his more substantial work, the novel *Báječná léta pod psa* ("Blissful Years of Lousy Living", 1992), he captured – with great sense of humour – the atmosphere of political dictatorship in which he himself grew up. As it was written when his country was free again after 1989, he could allow his irony and sarcasm to flow unrestrained, so that he saw, at times, a retrospect tragedy with tragicomic aspects.

In the novel *Výchova dívek v Čechách* ("Bringing up Girls in Bohemia", 1994, which was also filmed), about the narrator's love for the daughter of a *nouveau riche* father, the author exposes – again in a light, amusing vein – post 1989 social problems. While *Účastníci zájezdu* seems to be, so far, his most significant novel, Viewegh also published *Zapisovatelé otcovský lásky* ("Registrars of Paternal Love", 1998) and an earlier volume of parody on literature, *Nápady laskavého čtenáře* ("Ideas of a Kind Reader", 1993). Another book, *Báječná léta s Klausem* ("Blissful Years with Klaus"), came out in 2002, to be followed by *Vybíjená* ("A Ball Game") in 1994, registering the destinies of a few of his schoolmates.

## *Účastníci zájezdu*

Now in his forties, M. Viewegh is a Czech best-selling writer and his novels are not only widely read but also translated and even honoured (he received the Jiří Orten prize for his novel *Báječná léta pod psa)*. As the title *Účastníci zájezdu* indicates, one can expect to meet here a variety of people who have chosen the same holiday package at an Italian sea resort. Swimming, basking in the sun, eating and sleeping may not make a very exciting subject for a novel, but this one becomes more interesting as the author unfolds the stories of his fictional holidaymakers. Although the choice of the same vacation destination indicates similar interests, the participants' actions, both past and present, eventually form a colourful pattern.

Under the wing of an attractive, nineteen-year-old female guide, the company includes people from many different walks of life: a writer, a few literary critics, an MP, two female students, two homo-sexuals, several married couples, a teenage boy, two elderly ladies, an impecunious Ukrainian. All of them behave like tourists here, no matter what their place in normal life may be. The writer Max, the protagonist, has obviously joined the group in order to collect material for his next novel; having the components of his literary genre in mind all the time, he continually tells us what in fact he is doing: observing, compiling, criticizing, praising himself, as the case in each situation may be. Through this method, together with the author's keen sense of observation which brings even the most trivial events to life, a very readable novel takes shape.

As the characters interact, the writer believes that explicit sex is a must in a contemporary novel and wonders how to present the libido truthfully and convincingly yet avoid "slobbery pornog-raphy". This is a welcome signal to those readers who find reading about sex boring and tend to put away such reading; but, alas, some slobbering there must be, even if pornography has been kept away. During the week at the resort, several of the characters change bed partners, but at least there is a wedding in the offing, as befits the ending of a traditional novel. Sadly, the happy couple do not appear to be very much in love with each other; the ageing bride-to-be is seizing what is possibly her last chance, while the lonely Ukrainian engineer seems to be favourably inclined – all too true to life, perhaps, in a world where tender romance is disappearing.

Through the use of vivid interior monologues the author has wittily expressed the most private thoughts of his characters (the teenager's discovery that in fact he is *not* a homosexual, as he had thought, is one of the most amusing examples) and has concocted a lively story from comparatively trivial material: tourists do behave in a stereotypical way once on holiday. M. Viewegh has given them new individuality within this limited field.

In English

*Bringing up Girls in Bohemia,* A. G. Brain, trans., London, Readers International, 1997.

# SELECT BIBLIOGRAPHY

Unfortunately there are not many translations into English of the great old Czech classics, but Karel Čapek (1890–1938), who introduced the word 'robot' into the *Oxford English Dictionary*, was very popular in Britain in his lifetime: his works were translated almost immediately as they came out in Prague. These are now mostly out of print, but new translations are beginning to appear:

IN THE UNITED STATES: *Tales from Two Pockets*. Norma Comrada, trans., North Haven, CT, Catbird Press, 1994; *Apocryphal Tales,* Catbird Press, 1997; *Crossroads*, Norma Comrada, trans. Catbird Press, 2002; *Talks with T. G.Masaryk*, Michael Heim, trans., Catbird Press, 1995; *War with the Newts,* Ewald Osers, trans., Catbird Press, 1990;

IN GREAT BRITAIN: *Letters from England,* Geoffrey Newsome, trans., London, Claridge Press, 2001; *The Gardener's Year,* Geoffrey Newsome., trans., London, Claridge Press, 2003.

The following Further Reference list provides a good starting point for learning more about Czech fiction.

Jiří Kovtun, *Czech and Slovak Literature in English*, Washington, Library of Congress, 1984, 1988.

René Wellek, *Essays on Czech Literature,* The Hague, Mouton, 1963.

Leonard Klein, ed., *Encyclopedia of World Literature in the Twentieth Century,* 4 vols., New York, Frederick Ungar Publishing House, 1967–84.

Miloslav Rechcígl, jr., ed., *Czechoslovakia Past and Present,* The Hague, Mouton, 1968.

Arne Novák, *Czech Literature,* Peter Kussi, trans., supplement by W. E. Harkins, Ann Arbor, Michigan Slavic Publications, 1976.

W. E. Harkins, Paul Trenský, eds., *Czech Literature since 1956: a Symposium.* New York, Bohemica, 1980.

Bohuslava R. Bradbrook, *Karel Čapek, In Pursuit of Truth, Tolerance and Trust*, Brighton & Portland, Sussex Academic Press, 1998.

Robert Porter, *An Introduction to Twentieth Century Czech Fiction*, Brighton & Portland, Sussex Academic Press, 2001.

Robert B. Pynsent, *Czech Prose and Verse*, London, Athlone Press, University of London, 1979.

Alfred French, *Czech Writers and Politics, 1945–69*, Canberra, Australian National University Press, 1982.

Sam Solecki, *Prague Blues, The Achievement of Josef Škvorecký*, Toronto, ECW Press, 1990.

Sam Solecki, ed., *The Achievement of Josef Škvorecký*, Toronto, Buffalo, London, University of Toronto Press, 1994.

Michael Simmons, *The Reluctant President* (Václav Havel), London, Methuen, 1991.

Alexandra Büchler, ed., *This Side of Reality* (anthology), London, Serpent's Tail, 1996.

Elena Lappin, ed., *Daylight in Nightclub Inferno* (anthology), Czech Fiction from the Post-Kundera Generation, North Haven, CT, Catbird Press, 1997.

# INDEX

Note: + indicates works translated into English; bold types denote works dealt with in detail.

# INDEX

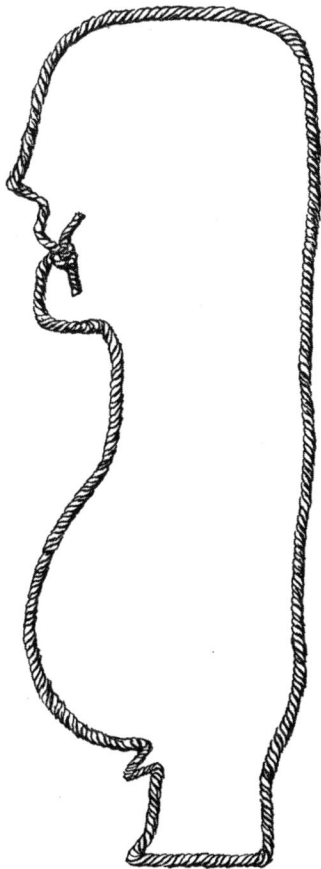

"Freedom of Speech under Communism"
From Jiří Jirásek, *Unás* (Prager Chronik)